# Soccer Thinking for Management Success

Though it may not have been apparent at first, I quickly learned that many of the principles and skills I learned on the soccer field and in the locker room directly applied to my new life in an office, handling and managing some of the brightest people I've ever met. Peter's book seamlessly brings both worlds together and shows just how similar they can be.

**Danny Karbassiyoon**, Co-Founder and Product Lead, PLAYRMAKR and Total Soccer: Road to Glory, author of *The Arsenal Yankee, first American to score at Arsenal*

You don't have to be a soccer fan to appreciate the lessons from *Soccer Thinking for Management Success*. This is a fun and interesting read that anyone who manages, or who one day wants to manage, will find helpful.

**Hon. Henry F. De Sio, Jr.**, 2008 COO of Obama for America and author of *Campaign Inc.: How Leadership and Organization Propelled Barack Obama to the White House*

I tell my management students the same thing I tell my soccer teams – communicate, support each other, and hold each other accountable. Peter captures these lessons and more in ways that show how thinking like a soccer player can help professionals succeed.

**Matt Winkler**, Director, Sports Analytics & Management, American University and Founder, The Sports Events Marketing Experience (The SEME), youth coach

"Soccer is war" Rinus Michels, the famed Dutch soccer coach, once said. Peter Loge doesn't go that far, but offers a highly original take on what business can learn from the addictive stew of tactical genius, technical brilliance and raw emotions that make soccer the world's most beautiful game.

**Friso van der Oord**, Director of Research, National Association of Corporate Directors; author of *Johan Cruyff, the American Years; aging soccer player and lifelong fan*

# Soccer Thinking for Management Success

# Soccer Thinking for Management Success

## Peter Loge

**CHANGE
MAKERS
BOOKS**

Winchester, UK
Washington, USA

First published by Changemakers Books, 2018
Changemakers Books is an imprint of John Hunt Publishing Ltd., No. 3 East Street,
Alresford, Hampshire SO24 9EE, UK
office1@jhpbooks.net
www.johnhuntpublishing.com
www.changemakers-books.com

For distributor details and how to order please visit the 'Ordering' section on our website.

ISBN: 978 1 78535 754 1
978 1 78535 755 8 (ebook)
Library of Congress Control Number: 2017948402

A CIP catalogue record for this book is available from the British Library.

Design: Stuart Davies

Printed and bound by CPI Group (UK) Ltd, Croydon, CR0 4YY, UK

We operate a distinctive and ethical publishing philosophy in
all areas of our business, from our global network of authors to
production and worldwide distribution.

# Contents

# Acknowledgments

This book would not exist were it not for my lovely young wife Zoë Beckerman, whose endless patience makes everything possible.

The whole project began as a series of conversations with Ben Olsen. Ben is among the kindest, most generous people I know. In addition to being a talented artist and good friend, he is one of the great American soccer figures of his generation. Emerson College classmate Brett Dewey provided editing, encouragement, ideas, and endless time to this and any number of other hair-brained ideas over the past 30-plus years. Another Emerson classmate, John Speaks, turned over his guest house to me so I could write (and then fed me at Hyperion Public, his bar in the Silver Lake neighborhood in Los Angeles). David Elliot regularly edits my political rants and took a red pen to this volume as well. Neil Richardson, who appears in this book, connected me to his publisher – without Neil this might be a series of blog posts read only by David and Brett. Countless other friends provided contacts, names, ideas, and encouragement. Thank you all.

Finally I need to thank those whose names appear in this book. A complete list of those folks, including their professional and soccer credentials, appears at the end. They range from World Cup winners and CEOs to middle managers and players whose careers peaked in local rec leagues. All of them were unreasonably generous with their time.

*Not a single day goes by in my work life as an entrepreneur that I don't use skills I learned playing soccer.*
Daniel Neal, CEO & Founder, Kajeet Inc. Former player, University of Rochester

# Foreword

Peter and I first talked about management after he had just begun a leadership position at a consulting firm and I was still a DC United midfielder. By then, I had played for a lot of coaches – in high school and college, for professional teams in England and the US, in the Olympics, and in the World Cup. Peter asked me what made a good coach from the player's perspective. I told him that as a player I wanted to know what was expected of me, I wanted clear and direct feedback, and I wanted to know the coach had my back.

We continued our management conversation after I became the coach of DC United and he had recently assumed a leadership role at the US Institute of Peace. I was learning how to manage soccer players at the same time Peter was navigating a new management role. We were amazed at the similarities in our jobs. Going back and forth on managing personalities, motivating a team, and creating the right culture. We share a belief that a group of professionals who get the little things right and who work hard for each other will succeed more often than not.

A coach in a lot of ways is a CEO. It's more than halftime speeches, game time adjustments, and training sessions. Managing up and down. Managing your own emotions. Creating the culture you desire. Communicating clearly. Media strategies. Being empathetic yet demanding. These are just as vital to the job as making the right substitution. And these are the aspects I believe are the real crossover in sports and business.

I found out very quickly in the unforgiving emotional world of coaching what my strengths and weaknesses were. At DC United I surround myself with people who make me whole. I focus on the character and grit of those I hire. I make sure they reflect the culture of the organization, and that they add to the success of the group. Then I try and give them the tools they need, and I let them do their job.

Peter's book expands these lessons, adds a few more, and ties them to situations he has faced as a manager and to situations faced by others. Not every management lesson from soccer can be applied to other organizations – you can't bench a CEO and bring him back when he is refocused, for example – but a lot of what makes a soccer team succeed day-in and day-out is akin to what makes a business organization succeed as well.

Soccer has taught both of us a lot when we let it. Hopefully some of what Peter and I have learned can help you as well.

Ben Olsen
Head Coach, DC United
Former professional player and member of the US Olympic and World Cup teams

# Introduction

The what, why, and structure of the book plus a few notes on language.

*Most organizations exist in a world where change is a constant; where interaction with allies and opponents is organic and unpredictable; where the success of the whole is founded upon the efforts and commitment of the several; where consistent preparation and empowerment can help increase the likelihood of desired outcomes.*

*That sounds exactly like the set of problems, and solutions, which soccer teams and clubs encounter and strive for. American football offers innumerable opportunities to stop play, evaluate situations, and recalibrate responses – but increasingly that approach is less and less relevant to the dynamic changes in business or society. The rules are being rewritten every day – or every hour – and the ability to quickly adapt has never been more important.*

Kevin Payne, CEO US Club Soccer, one of the founders of Major League Soccer, former President and CEO of D.C. United and former President and General Manager of Toronto FC, and long-time US Soccer Board member.

Organizational success used to look like football. Today it looks like soccer.

Expertise is no longer confined to a couple of smart guys in corner offices, reviewing information to which only they have access and issuing instructions through layers of middlemen to nine-to-fivers who carry out the dictates and feed paper back up the chain to await the next set of instructions. Today's world is networked and always working. Organizations no longer have the luxury of time. Everyone in today's successful organization has a role and a specialty, and everyone fills in for everyone else. Managers fix copiers and drivers deliver breakthrough innovations. Success is no longer football, with its series of discreet plays and fixed roles. Gone is the coach issuing instructions to a quarterback who relays those instructions to a constantly shifting assortment of specialists whose lives are devoted to one and only one task. Organizational success requires real-time decision making, independent action, and systems thinking. Organizational success is now soccer.

In football the coach and his assistants plan a play and get it to the quarterback. The quarterback gathers his players to explain the instructions and everyone heads to the line of scrimmage and runs the play. At the end of the play the game stops, the coaches evaluate the situation and send in another play. The same thing happens on defense – the defensive coordinator reviews the action from the sidelines and swaps players and formations as he sees fit. The plays are fixed sets of actions, each of which are drawn out in notebooks and practiced during the week.

In football, players do and coaches think. Coaches swap in and out specialists based on the needs of the position and needs of the play. Players are expected to only do what their position and specialty dictate. Players are interchangeable gears in a complex machine run by others.

Soccer is very different than football. Once play starts it only stops for injuries, fouls and when the ball goes out of bounds. Stoppages are typically short, timewasters are punished, and the time lost is made up at the end of each half. The average football game has about 11 minutes of action over an hour of playing time, and usually consumes over three hours when you factor in halftime and commercial breaks. Soccer games are 90 minutes of action in 90 minutes of playing time with one 15-minute halftime. There are no TV timeouts. Soccer referees do not stop play if calling a foul would hurt the team fouled. Soccer is systems thinking in action.

In soccer, as in other sports, there is a coach that sets the strategy and decides who does what, but once the game starts the coach is relegated to making three personnel changes and yelling from the sideline. In soccer those who decide, also do. Roles are less fixed in soccer than in football. The goalkeeper is the only one allowed to use his hands, and even then only within a fixed area. Everyone is expected to do everything. Forwards attack and defenders defend – and forwards also defend and defenders also attack. Goalkeepers occasionally score.

I have managed a division of a private company, a division of a federally funded organization, an advocacy organization, and a Congressional office. I have served on management committees and was a presidentially-appointed member of the federal Senior Executive Service, advising the Commissioner of the US Food and Drug Administration. For seven years I was an independent strategic communications and political consultant, building and managing teams as needed.

I am also a soccer guy. I have had season tickets to DC United (my local pro team) since the league in which they play was founded, and I am a third-generation Arsenal Football Club fan. I have served on the boards of soccer charities and helped organize a grassroots effort to get a new stadium for DC United. I have been to sleep-away soccer camp more often as an adult (twice) than as a kid (once), and I have played both pick-up and recreational league soccer in and around Washington for more years than my knees care to count.

A few years ago I started applying what I learned from soccer to the office. I have explained my management-as-soccer approach to soccer fans and non-fans, and more often than not the ideas struck a chord. The lessons in this book are derived from what I have learned as a player and fan, what I have learned from Ben Olsen, a friend who is a professional coach and retired player, from friends who are similarly soccer people and managers, from the interviews I did specifically for this book, and from the writings of others on management, soccer, and sports. Hopefully these lessons will help you as they have helped me, even if your knowledge of soccer is that it is a big deal everywhere else and that David Beckham somehow matters.

Just as success in soccer requires everyone on the team, this book is intended for everyone in an organization – not just those who tell others what to do or those who are expected to do as they are told. The book has a consistent structure and works largely deductively. Every chapter begins with a clever quote or two and has a few highlighted quotes and examples that help demonstrate the point of the chapter. I then explain an area of soccer that highlights the point of the chapter, followed by a discussion of how those lessons apply to organizations and management. At the end of every chapter I offer a few key "locker room notes" that distill the lessons into points that can be written on a white board in an office. I also offer ideas on how to put the ideas into practice.

The book goes from big ideas, to smaller ideas, to even smaller ones (and as a result relatively longer chapters down to relatively shorter ones, which has the added advantage of making it feel as if you are reading quickly). I start with the whole team as a system idea, then turn to major component parts of that system, and finally at smaller pieces of insight that support the whole.

This book is only part of the project and conversation. This book focuses on how what goes on the field can help improve what goes on in the office. But there is much more of the story to tell. More essays, ideas, and insights are at www. SoccerThinking.com. There you also will find guest posts by soccer and management people, videos, thoughts from weekend games and headlines, and more. For example, the website looks at how soccer is handling racism and homophobia on and off the field, and what private companies can learn from those efforts. The website also looks at elements of the complex industry that has become soccer and all that goes in to making a team succeed, from bringing young players and managing talent through the youth ranks to building and maintaining a global brand.

## Notes on language

*America and England are two nations separated by a common language.*
Attributed to Oscar Wilde and George Bernard Shaw

Like most subcultures soccer has its own language. And like most subcultures that feel besieged or marginalized (as US soccer fans are wont to do) people can get testy about using the right words to demonstrate you "get it." For the passionate, fields are pitches, cleats are boots, uniforms are kits, games are matches, and a game between local rivals is called a "derby" (pronounced "darby").

People can get especially exercised about "football" versus "soccer." They will shout until they are blue in the face that Americans should call it football along with the rest of the world – the game is played with the feet after all. My calling it soccer here may make some readers roll their eyes, but at least everyone will know what I'm talking about. Calling it football all the way through only makes things more confusing, so I ask the purists for their indulgence (and I would remind them that "soccer" is actually a British word for the sport, not some goofy American invention). The exception to this rule is when I am quoting someone else directly and the meaning of the word is clear from the context, which mostly means sometimes "football" means "soccer."

Tackle is one term that is important to soccer and (American) football that may cause confusion. Most of us know that a football tackle is a defender dragging down someone carrying the ball. A soccer tackle is someone taking the ball from someone else, and given the rules of the game doesn't typically result in the guy with the ball going face first into the turf. A defender tackles the ball away from a forward by sticking his leg or foot in.

*The rules of soccer are very simple, basically it is this: if it moves, kick it. If it doesn't move, kick it until it does.*

Phil Woosnam, former Welsh player and commissioner of the original North American Soccer League, "Phil Woosman, Pioneer of North American Soccer Dies at 80"

With that, game on!

# Chapter 1

# It Takes a Team

A soccer team is a system made up of 11 parts that interact to ensure the success of the whole. Modern organizations are also systems made up of staff and managers working together for a shared goal.

> *Always play for your team, never for yourself or for the amusement of the spectators.*
> Hubert Vogelsinger, How to Star in Soccer

> *Venture capital firms invest in teams, so you need to be a team worth investing in.*
> Danny Karbassiyoon, Co-Founder and Product Lead, SWOL/ Fury90, former Arsenal player

A team is a system in which each part works with, and for, the other parts.

Successful soccer teams are not collections of superstars who do not pass the ball or players who show flashes of brilliance but who are otherwise unreliable. Successful soccer teams are groups in which skilled players are in their best positions and who work together as a single unit toward a shared goal. In 2016 a team in England called Leicester City – which barely survived being demoted to a lower division at the end of the 2014/2015 season – beat 5,000 to one odds to finish as the best team in England. When Leicester's star was playing semi-professional soccer a few years before winning it all, second-place Arsenal players were winning the World Cup. In the same season the talent-stacked Chelsea, defending Premier League champion with a payroll of roughly $310 million, finished 10th, not much better than Bournemouth – a team that had a payroll of roughly $38 million and which spent much of its 70-year history in the third division of English soccer.[1] Leicester and Bournemouth (and Arsenal) did well in part because they were teams, not just collections of expensive stars. They moved as a unit, worked for each other, and were fully committed to the system and goal. Chelsea did poorly in part because the team's stars did not work together, for each other, or for their manager, Jose Mourinho. Before he was fired mid-season, Mourinho (who calls himself "the special one") publicly criticized his players for betraying him. One of his players – on international television – threw a shirt at Mourhino; the shirt fell just short of its target, summing up the team's season.

> …teamwork is the most striking thing about the side, and has enabled them to possess that most valuable commodity in the Championship [England's second division] – winning while playing badly.–
> ESPN FC on Brighton, which had just won promotion to the top division in England from the second-tier Championship division

My local team, DC United, has historically had among the lowest payrolls in Major League Soccer. Unlike virtually every other team in the league, as of 2017 DC United has had no stars from the top leagues in Europe and it has been a while since DC United players were regular starters for the US Men's National Team. For at least a decade it has been a collection of hardworking and solid players from around MLS and some young talent coming up through the system. Yet the team regularly advances in the playoffs, spends time at or near the top of the league standings, and Ben Olsen was Coach of the Year in 2014. In the second decade of the 21st century DC United was usually known for being hard-working, not having a lot of flash, and being hard to beat.

*The best way to win is to play football where everybody expresses his talent. What is marvelous in this game ... nobody has all the qualities, but in a team sport what is very interesting is to develop the strong qualities of each player and to put a harmony [on top] and put that to work together and then be efficient as a unit. What is marvelous in the game is 1+1+1 is more than 11. When you manage to do that, you have built a team. That will be a team with style because everybody expresses his qualities. And that will be a team that is efficient because everybody brings his best to the unit.*
Arsenal Manager Arsene Wenger, Arseblog

The same principal of teamwork beating freelancing stars at the very top level is also true of casual weekend pickup games and local rec league play. Everyone wants to be on a team that wins, but no one wants a teammate who won't pass the ball or defend. People want to play on teams that behave like teams – teams that ensure everyone is involved in the play, teams on which everyone works as hard on defense as they do at scoring, teams that recognize everyone has to take a turn playing goalkeeper if need be. If stars do not involve other players, other players stop involving the stars. The predicable result is that the team loses.

*There are occasions when you have to ask yourself whether certain players are affecting the dressing-room atmosphere, the performance of the team, and your control of the players and staff. If they are, you have to cut the cord. There is absolutely no other way. It doesn't matter if the person is the best player in the world. The long-term view of the club is more important than any individual ...*
Sir Alex Ferguson, former head coach of Manchester United, "Ferguson's Forumula"

The best organizational teams, like the best soccer teams, are made up of people who work with and for each other. A former senior leader at an international health system explains the importance of teams in operating rooms and hospitals in general: To ensure the safety of the patient, everyone in the operating room needs to know what they are supposed to do and do it well – and they also have to know what everyone else is doing and why so they can adjust as necessary. This is true beyond the operating room and extends to the entire hospital – in one of the places in which she worked the CEO knew everyone's name and their contribution to the organization's success, from senior administrator to maintenance staff. One result was that the organization ran as a team with everyone working together. She contrasted this to a hospital she was sent to help improve in which "if the CEO knew a dozen people's names I'd be surprised." The CEO not only didn't know the names and roles of those on whom the hospital's success relied, he never even saw many of them – he took a private elevator from the garage to his office. In this system there were groups of individuals working individually, but they were not working together as a team. As a result the hospital was not doing well, and was never going to get better.

We have all worked at companies that put up with the staff member who is typically a slouch (at best) but who shows flashes of brilliance. We know about (or have worked for) the prima donna who thinks the success of the company is all because of him but failure is the fault of the staff. And we have all been in meetings where a few people try to prove they are the smartest in the room and as a result ensure that other voices are not heard and the best ideas may not be pursued. No one wants to work with those people, to support their efforts, or even be in the same room with them. These staff members may have great moments or have occasional magical insight, but the toll they take on the organization means the occasional victories are outweighed by the missed opportunities and overall underperformance caused by a team not consistently working together. The amount of time and effort it takes to put up with these solo artists, and the numbers of colleagues who simply will not work with these non-team players, detracts from success more than it adds. Flashy and self-promoting colleagues may get attention, but too often they do not get organizational results.

Management literature is full of studies proving this point. Famous or flashy CEOs do not do as well as their less famous counterparts, and their counterparts typically cost a lot less. Collections of leaders with big egos tend to devolve into arguments among themselves, or worse engage in individual efforts that intentionally avoid coordination and undermine the work of others and the goals of the team. The best companies are like the best soccer teams – good people who become great when working together. The work may not be flashy and might not result in gushing profiles in business magazines, but the work is very, very good.

*You want to build a culture in which everyone fights for each other.* Danny Karbassiyoon, Co-Founder and Product Lead SWOL/ Fury90, former Arsenal player

The best companies, like the best teams, are not made up of the best individual performers. The best companies, like the best teams, are made up of the most effective teammates, each of whom is good at his or her role and is also good at supporting others in their roles.

One challenge is that companies with stars, egos, and poor teamwork often do well. It is not as if stars with egos are bad at what they do – the ego is often justified. As a result companies at which they work (and teams on which they play) often do well. They just do not do as well as others or as well as they could. DC United's hardworking band of underpaid players no one has heard of won games, but they have not won the championship with this group. Leicester City had its moment but it has since fallen back to earth and Chelsea is back on top (with a new coach). In addition, firms or companies that rely on stars may not be able to survive the departure of that star. The focus on the star may have prevented a strong organization able to survive the person from developing, or the personality overwhelms the organization entirely. Either way, it is bad news for the organization. The best leaders embrace the admonition often attributed to Charles de Gaulle that "the graveyards are full of indispensable men."

## Locker Room Notes for Managers

Do not hire or tolerate selfish staff. Seek out and reward good team players. Take the time to look behind self-promotional efforts, and look for the work of those who do not draw attention to themselves.

Remind your staff that you measure success against the shared goal of the organization and against the unit's own goals – you do not reward attention-getting or bragging by individuals, you reward measurable results of the team. Then reward them as such.

Focus on the team to avoid falling into "the special one" trap. By putting individual goals in the context of advancing team goals and providing feedback on performance of a staff member's behavior in the context of team goals and impact on other members of the team, managers can help improve team performance. By focusing on team goals and team results in meetings, managers reinforce the value of group results (rather than individual performances). One way to ensure you do this, and that everyone hears you doing it, is to start with the goal and team before talking about an individual – the difference between "increasing staff retention is a team goal this year, one way we're doing that is informal mentorship of junior staff, Denise has done a great job of working with two new hires" and "Denise is doing a great job by taking two new hires under her wing" can be massive. The former is about the team in which an individual is playing a part; the latter is only about the individual.

## Locker Room Notes for Staff

Be a team player. Ensure you are doing as well as you can at the role you are assigned, know and understand others' roles and find ways to help support others in their assigned roles.

Put your work in the context of advancing unit and organizational goals when talking about your work with your supervisor; talk about the progress of the team toward the goal and the role you played on the team rather than talking about your individual successes. If we have learned anything from post-game press conferences it is that one should thank one's team and talk about the importance of a team's success rather than individual success. In meetings, publicly call out colleagues who contribute to the team by leading with a team goal: "As a team, we committed to mentoring new staff and increasing retention. Denise is helping the team do this ..."

## Endnotes

1.  In England, as in most soccer leagues around the world, there are a number of tiers of leagues from amateur, through semi-professional, to a few professional leagues. In most countries at the end of each season the top teams in each division get promoted and the teams at the bottom get demoted. In England there are 24 official divisions with a total of 483 leagues.

## Chapter 2

# Total Football

Modern soccer teams move as a unit. Players have specialties, but everyone is expected to do everything as needed. Modern organizations are the same. Staff are hired for their specific skills, but must be willing and able to fill other roles as well.

*The new tiki-taka style created constantly changing strategies and passing combinations, making movements difficult to predict. Defenders find it difficult to cover players, their constant passing ...Players interact by passing, using each pass to communicate intuitively with a teammate, the "we" superseding the "me." Tiki-taka-style swarm intelligence has thus become the offense's answer to the complexity of modern defenses.*
Wolfgang Jenewein, Thomas Kochanek, Marcus Heidbrink and Christian Schimmelpfennig, "Learning Collaboration from Tiki-Taka Soccer"

*One of the beauties of the Dutch "Total Football" philosophy was that players weren't limited to thinking, "My job is to be the best defender or the best mid-fielder." Instead, they were focused on moving the ball forward collectively, creating scoring chances, and ultimately winning the game.*

*Likewise, when you encourage members of your organization to stop thinking solely in the bounds of their departments and individual roles (ex: my job is to provide x amount of leads, or produce x lines of code), then you open up more opportunities for them to contribute to moving the needle, sometimes in ways you may not even anticipate.*
Jonathan Crowe, "Agile Lessons from the Most Innovative Team in World Cup History"

Successful organizations, like successful soccer teams, are systems in which everyone has a specific role and in which everyone sometimes fills the roles of others. Everyone works for and with everyone else. The single-skill specialist who only does one thing is increasingly obsolete, while those with the most value are those who excel at one thing and who can do a variety of other tasks well. Everyone is an autonomous decision maker, using his or her best judgment about what is needed to advance the goal. Because systems are complex and no one can see or process all of the parts of it at once, everyone in the system has to constantly share information and process information shared by others. The authors whose quotes open this chapter compare contemporary soccer to the "hive mind" approach to problem solving.

The legendary Dutch teams of the 1970s led by Johann Cruyff developed a style of play called Total Football. It required players to go beyond their traditional roles as forwards who only attacked and defenders who only defended. Under this new system, players had to do a bit of everything. Everyone moved forward together and everyone moved back together. When the play was on the left side of the field, the whole unit shifted left. When the play shifted right, so did the players. This system often relied on players using lots of short passes, called tika-taka after the sound the ball makes when it is being passed quickly.

*In my teams, striker is first defender and goalie is the first attacker.* Johan Cruyff, legendary player and manager, "A tribute to Johan Cruyff, the Dutch soccer maestro"

An example of total commitment to a team rather just to an assigned role is US National Team player Carli Lloyd's performance in the final of the 2015 Women's World Cup against Japan. Lloyd, a forward, put three goals past Japan in a span of 16 minutes, essentially deciding the game before halftime. And still, in the final minutes of a game the US was leading 5-2, Lloyd ran all the way back on defense to help out her teammates. Lloyd was on the field to score goals, which she did. She was also there to help in the midfield and on defense as part of a system that required all of the players to always be aware and able to go where they were needed most. Her actions as a specialist in attack and supporter on defense did more than score goals and prevent Japan from scoring. Her actions set and reflected the approach of the entire team.

For the system to work everyone must be good at their primary task and also be able to do the jobs of others on the field. The successful system further requires that everyone on the field be aware of where their teammates and opponents are, constantly look for threats and opportunities, and communicate problems and solutions while simultaneously moving to take advantage of those opportunities (or help their teammates to take advantage of them) and counter the threats (or help their teammates counter them).

Successful soccer coaches are strong leaders. The team has to believe in and support the coach's approach. Coaches have to inspire their teams to give a little bit more when games are not going well, and they need to keep players focused when a game seems easy. A lot of successful coaching is management, the logistics of the game. Soccer coaches gather information on upcoming opponents, establish the game plan, set the lineup, and determine who will be subbed in and out during the game, all while keeping an eye on the larger needs of the team throughout the season. Coaches know when to rest players and when to push them, who needs a pep talk and who needs to be shouted at. They are the CEOs of the team. The best coaches also know that once a game starts, success requires letting leaders emerge in the moment as the moment demands it.

A friend named Sarah Warren who played college soccer and who has held senior leadership positions at several international organizations identifies distributed leadership as being necessary in total football and in modern organizations. As she puts it:

> People can lead from the front, from the behind, from the side ... they might lead in one play but hang back on another ... they might be a veteran player or a rookie. If you're playing well as a team, leadership is distributed and fluid.

> *[Embassy staff] did what needed to be done, even if it was not their area of expertise. It is like the concept of 'total football'; everyone had a role in the Embassy but if people needed to do beyond that, that is what the team did.*
> Ambassador Arturo Sarukhan, Mexican Ambassador to the United States 2007–2013

Organizations increasingly need people who see the entire organization, who can identify and act on threats and opportunities, and who are willing and able to do more than what may have been in the job description. Engineers must be willing and able to think about market opportunities for products, and marketers should be thinking about ways products can work better. Organizations need specialists who can think like generalists when needed, who can lead when called upon, who can follow when necessary, and who are comfortable as independent decision makers acting in the larger system of independent decision makers.

Organizations are often set up in ways that set goals in isolation. Sales teams are judged on sales, architects on plans, and lawyers on hours. But sales only succeed if the product is something a customer values, architectural plans should become houses, and billed hours should become client victories. These broader goals require managers and staff to focus not just on what they were hired to do, but also on the larger goal of the company or firm. Sales staff should provide feedback to the marketing team and those doing the manufacturing should provide feedback to designers. Architects should help clients build additions, which means knowing how to manage projects as well as design them. The economic model of law firms is increasingly tenuous and good lawyers need to find ways to help their clients solve problems – of which the law may only be a part.

*You need to connect every job to the overall goal.*
Ari Gejdenson, CEO and Founder Mindful Restaurants Group and former professional soccer player

In 2013 I was brought in as the first vice president for external relations for the US Institute of Peace (USIP), an organization set up and largely funded by Congress. Before the creation of my position, the communications team worked largely independently from the team charged with managing relationships with Congress. These teams worked independently from those managing strategic relationships with other federal agencies, from the development team, and from the public education team. All of the teams worked in parallel with the rest of the Institute, more or less, but were not integrated into the work itself. My task was to take five largely autonomous teams, plus a new program, and integrate them into a single strategic unit that itself was fully a part of the work of USIP. My directors and I went through USIP's strategic plan and found all the places that applied to us. We identified our goals, and wrote a plan to achieve them as a team. Then each team wrote a strategic plan for its unit, identifying how each would advance these goals. The teams shared their plans and found ways to support each other. We created a shared calendar, a shared workflow system, and a shared document system so everyone could work seamlessly with each other. The directors met weekly to talk about what was coming up, challenges they were facing, help they needed, and help they had to offer. I moved as much of my team as would fit into the same space, and put up a big-screen monitor in an open area that was split between Twitter feeds and a shared calendar that showed major organizational deadlines and events as well as the travel schedule of staff. I hired a junior staff member who reported to me, but who worked for the team doing what was needed in the moment.

We created a system that supported the larger system of the Institute. The integrated team made measurable progress toward the Institute's strategic plan, made measureable progress toward its own internal goals, and helped the other teams at USIP achieve their goals. The team was playing total football, moving as a unit, leading and following, always in support of each other and advancing the ultimate goal.

*Well coach, that's not my position but I'll do the best I can — Ave Maria University player when asked to take on an unfamiliar role.* Antonio Soave, Former Kansas Secretary of Commerce, Chairman and CEO of Capistrano Global Advisory Services, former head coach at Ave Maria University in Florida and Franciscan University of Steubenville in Ohio, and former semi-professional player.

If a staff member is unwilling to shift roles to help the organization reach its goals, the staff member probably should not work at the organization. A friend who runs a technology company and who grew up playing soccer told me he had to let someone go because she was unwilling to take on different responsibilities. "Can you imagine if a coach told a forward to play defense," he asked, "and the player said 'no, I'm just a forward'?" A player who refuses to play a different role either finds himself on the bench or playing another sport. The same is true for staff.

## Locker Room Notes for Mangers

Make sure everyone on your team knows how the team's work advances the organization's goals, and the role they each play in advancing those goals. Everyone on your team should be able to clearly state what they are doing at any moment to support the team and organization goals.

Reward staff who help out on projects as needed, even if the help they are providing is not their specific skill set or what they are best at; everyone can proofread, everyone can answer a phone. Reward team support.

## Locker Room Notes for Staff

Be a total staffer.

Be sure you can always draw a clear line from what you are doing to your team's goals and your organization's goals. If you cannot always draw that line, work with your manager to clarify both the goals and you and your teammate's roles in advancing toward those goals.

Find ways to help your colleagues accomplish their goals in the context of the organization's goals.

## Chapter 3

# Know the System, Play Your Role

Soccer teams succeed if everyone knows the system and plays their role. Managers and staff must similarly know the organizational structure, know their role in that structure, and fulfill that role.

*Once you take the field with 10 other players, your first thought should always be for the team. A team of 11 good players, working together, will always beat a team of 11 disorganized all-stars. Each player should know precisely what's expected of him and what he can expect from his teammates. The result is a smooth, strong offense and defense. You can't win without either.*
Hubert Vogelsinger, How to Star in Soccer

*When a team works in harmony the player does not need to look for teammates...The coordination as part of a strategy and tactics should make a player always be in the position where the midfielder is going to aim for the pass; in the right spot where the wing is going to hang the ball in the box; in the exact place where the forward can let the ball go for the teammate to take the shot. It is the same in organizations. Strategy and the tactics need to be shared for the team to work in harmony and everyone in the organization should be in a position to take advantage of what their colleagues are doing.*
Ander Caballero, Delegate of the Basque Country to the United States, former COO Progenika, former amateur soccer player

A team playing total football only works if there is a system, and everyone knows their role in that system. That there is a system to soccer may come as a surprise to readers whose primary exposure to the game is watching a mass of kids chase a ball (and the occasional butterfly or puppy). If this is you, I encourage you to find a professional game on TV or online; watch not just the player with the ball but how all of the other players move as well. Soccer teams will line up with three or four at the back, four or five in the midfield, and one or two players up front. In soccer-speak these are 3-5-2, 4-4-2, 4-5-1, and so forth (the numbers only add up to 10 and not 11 because the one in goal is taken for granted so the goalkeeper isn't counted). The system moves together, with everyone playing a role and with everyone having a responsibility to the system itself. By working as a system the players are able to maximize their strengths and compensate for their weaknesses, while simultaneously minimizing their opponent's strengths and exploiting their opponent's weaknesses.

Not all systems are good fits for all players and not all players are a good fit for all systems. Systems that rely on chasing down long passes and running past slower defenders need to have players who can hit long, accurate passes and fast players who can chase those passes down. On the other hand, systems that rely on intricate passes to get through the opposition's defenses need players who can pass accurately in tight spaces, but who may not need to be able to make repeated sprints up and down the field. Good passers who aren't that fast would fail in the former system, and players whose primary skill is speed are a poor fit for the latter.

Jamie Vardey was a player few had heard of before he broke the record for scoring in consecutive games in the English Premier League in 2015. Vardey played for an English team unfamiliar with top flight success, the Leicester City Football Club, and until a few years earlier he was a semi-professional in the fifth division of English soccer, working in a factory to make ends meet. Leicester finished the 2015/16 season in first place while the legendary Manchester United finished fifth. One of

Manchester United's problems was that they were not scoring a lot of goals. It would be tempting to suggest that Man U (as they are sometime called) should have tried to buy Vardey from Leicester. Tempting, but a mistake. One reason Vardey scored so much is because he was the right guy for Leicester's system – he is tall, runs onto the ball, and is good at receiving long passes. He was also surrounded by supporting players who got him the ball when and where he could do the most with it. Vardey's success was due in part to his playing in the right system with the right players around him. Man U played a different system, one that relied on a slow and deliberate attack, a system in which Vardey would likely not have had the same success. It is telling that the following season Leicester lost one of their top midfielders to Chelsea, a player named N'Golo Kante whose job at Leicester was to get Vardey the ball. Kante thrived at Chelsea. He was named the league's Player of the Year and Chelsea won the title, while Vardey's and Leicester's fortunes fell.

> *"What is most important is that the system takes advantage of the quality of the players individually as much as possible," [Arsenal manager Arsene] Wenger told the club's official website … [Whether or not change the system for a single player is] "a dilemma for the Arsenal manager to ponder – and highlights the difficulty in recruiting 'top, top quality' players who fit your system and style."*
> Peter Smith, "Where would Riyad Mahrez fit in at Arsenal?"

Professional soccer coaches have a lot of leeway in who they sign and who they cut, and who they play and who they bench. But even professional sports teams have limits to what they can do. The league may impose a salary cap, owners have limits in what they are willing to spend, and there is a limited pool of players from which to choose. Because soccer fields are different sizes coaches have to adjust for their home-field confines. Because soccer is played in lots of different climates coaches have to account for the impact that weather makes – you can run more in cold and dry conditions than in hot and humid or rainy ones. Teams play differently at Mexico City's Estadio Azetca that is 7,200 feet above sea level than they do at London's Wembley Stadium that sits 187 feet above sea level. Culture also matters, different countries develop different styles; some teams and leagues are largely dominated by people from those countries, while others are melting pots of languages and ways of approaching the game. A good coach looks at his players, considers the local conditions, knows what he can change and what he can't, and finds the system that puts his players in the best position to succeed.

A good example of succeeding under these sorts of constraints is a team in the Spanish leagues called Athletic de Bilbao (or Bilboko Athletic Kluba in Basque). Bilbao is the primary team of the biggest city in the passionately independent Basque region of Spain. Bilbao only signs players from the Basque country or who are of Basque heritage. This limits the pool of potential players because there are only about two million people in the Basque country (roughly the population of New Mexico). Bilbao has to find the right system for the players and the right players for the system because they do not have the luxury of signing the best stars in the world. To put it in perspective, Lionel Messi, the only player to ever win the Ballon d'Or award for the best player in the world five times, is an Argentine who plays for Barcelona – the only other player to win the award between 2008 and 2015 was Christiano Ronaldo, a Portuguese player at Real Madrid, both rival teams in the same league as Bilbao. Bilbao still manages to regularly finish high enough in the standings to qualify for one of the major European tournaments. They may not have deep pockets, but they have a good system and committed approach.

Rec league soccer has even more limitations. You tend to play with the people who make it to the game on time, who are healthy enough to play, and whose checks for league fees clear. Rec league teams also have official or unofficial captains, someone whose job is both administrative (collect the money for the league fees, fill out the appropriate forms, remind players that game is coming up) and strategic (deciding who plays where, who gets substituted[1] and when, and so forth). As often as not the person who collects the money is the captain or manager, or he appoints someone to that role. While it is nearly impossible to fire a volunteer player – I am not sure I have ever been on a rec league team that cut someone – you can recruit new players to add depth or replace those who leave the team.[2] As a rec league team captain you have some hiring ability, but no firing ability. You work with what you've got and what you can go get.

Pickup soccer is even more limited with teams being decided based on who shows up. Pickup soccer does not have a coach or captain. Good players quickly figure out where they can be most useful, what system makes the most sense for the number of people on the side, and slot themselves in.[3] Groups of experienced players create a system that increases the chances of the team's success. To repeat a theme that runs through this book, pickup soccer players talk to each other a lot to sort themselves out. If someone has been playing forward a lot, or running up and back in the midfield, he may drop back and tell a defender to go forward both so he can rest and also out of fairness. Similarly a defender may ask a midfielder or forward to drop back for a bit so she can play a more attacking role. For example, if you're in a 4v4 game, players will either assume or quickly decide to form a diamond with one at the back, one at the front and the other two on the sides. If there are five of you, you may decide to keep two back and have the other three form a triangle in front of them. Players often voice strengths and weaknesses or simply drop into those positions. This ad hoc group with a shared mission comes together and quickly determines the organizational system that is most likely to lead to success.

*Most five-a-side players like to do a bit of everything with no fixed positions: total football, they often call it, though opponents prefer another two-word phrase: easy pickings.*

*"Like the 11-a-side game, you do have options when it comes to picking the right formation," says [Arsenal Manager] Arsene [Wenger]. "You can play two at the back, one in midfield and one up front, or you can have one attacker and three defenders but I would suggest a formation that nicely marries defence with attack ... On the face of it, my recommended formation is 1-2-1. One defender, one attacker, with two what I would call offensive full-backs. These two players should fall back and defend when you don't have the ball but be ready to get forward and attack when necessary."*

Arsenal Manager Arsene Wenger "Wenger: How to Improve Your Five-a-Side" (the numbers add up to four because the fifth is assumed to be a goalkeeper who does not get counted in the formation).

Regardless of the level, teams do best when players stick to their roles. Players need to know that teammates will be where they are supposed to be. A forward needs to stay forward, so if a defender kicks the ball up field there is someone to receive it – if the forward isn't where he is supposed to be, the opposing team will just launch another attack. Similarly, the central defender needs to stay on defense and cannot join every attack because someone needs to make sure there is a line of protection if the other team wins the ball and starts a counter attack. One advantage of soccer as a system is that if the assigned person is out of position, someone else slides in so that the role is filled; the system continues to function because everyone knows the pieces of that system and works to ensure those pieces are in place at all times.

A feature of a good team is that it sticks to the system, regardless of the events of the moment. Players "keep their shape" in soccer-speak. A player unilaterally opting out of a system, or players chucking the plan out the window without a new plan, can be disastrous. Eleven organized players are always better than 11 guys running around doing stuff. Good teams may adjust the system to meet unexpected challenges or demands; the system adapts under the coach's guidance. The change is intentional and system-wide. Good teams "work their way" back into games by focusing on their system and players executing their roles. These teams sometimes win, often tie, and when they lose the damage is not as bad as it might have been. Bad teams take early setbacks as cause for abandoning the system; players second-guess the coach and do as they please, or second-guess their teammates and either attack their own players or ignore their teammates and try to do everything themselves. This almost always ends poorly.

*A team can be out-possessed, out-shot, etc. ... but the team with the most discipline to the game plan can emerge victorious, even when overmatched. It's similar to the working world. When an organization stays true to their values and is strategic in planning, they can navigate challenges and achieve their goals. The day-to-day can often be filled with chaos and crisis. The composure and poise that our organization possesses helps us move through these times of unrest successfully.*

Tanya Vogel, Senior Associate Athletics Director, The George Washington University, former player and head coach at GW, member of the GW Athletics Hall of Fame

It is easy to see how players abandoning a system in panic could be disastrous. Less obvious is that success can have the same effect. We have all watched teams in almost every sport jump to what seemed like an insurmountable lead, only to collapse and fail. Inevitably the team worked well within their system, got a lead, then either got lazy or began to ignore the system in favor of individuals showing off. While the team in the lead drifted out of the system that got them there, the team they were beating either stuck to their system or adjusted to a new one and relentlessly played it, knowing that players working for each other can almost always beat players working only for themselves.

Your role in the system on the field is only part of your responsibility as a player. You also need to know your role on the team. You may need to be the vocal captain, the calm and steady presence, the "super sub" who comes in late to change the game, or the older player who may not get on the field as much but whose experience can help when called upon. On my 45+ team my role is that of an energetic, hard running defender, but when I play pickup or on a team with no age restrictions, my role is typically as the person who can hit a decent long pass, defend physically, and can put in a few minutes of calm, conservative play when needed. If I didn't play aggressively and run hard on my over-45 team I would be failing to fulfill my role just as much as if I tried to sprint around 20-somethings on younger teams.

The CEO of a medium-sized organization asked if I would join him and a few of his senior staff for coffee to talk about their strategic plan. The organization was 25 years old, and he had been in his current role for about a year. The strategic plan set bold goals that would be met with focus and collaboration. Under the new plan, the organization was going to behave differently, it was going to operate in a different system. He wanted my help in thinking about how to explain this new approach to the outside world and wanted my thoughts on how to manage for the new approach. A challenge was that while the work was explained as collaborative, each stream feeding and being fed by the next, the organizational chart remained static and siloed. He had a good game plan, but the wrong system. Until he addressed the system question he could not address other management issues. With the system set, the explanation to the outside world is easier because the system itself is doing the work which the organization wants to talk about.

It seems obvious that an organization needs a system, but I have had enough conversations with managers and would-be managers to know that they say the word "system" a lot but really mean "org chart." People show up for work and do their job. If an employee manages others, she goes about managing them. When someone leaves or a new position is created the manager thinks about replacing that person or filling that role. A manager may think "how will this new person work with others?" but that is only in the context of the individual, "cultural fit" or how will this new marble bump off the other marbles already in the box? The thought should be "what system do I want, and what hard and soft skills do I therefore need to make that system work?" Rather than think about the impact of the new marble, think about how and in what direction you want the collection of marbles to move together. Cultural fit and personality are part of that, but only part. At least as important is what that person's skill set and approach will bring to the whole, and if the entire team can be shifted into a new system which would help inform who the new hire should be.

Try this quick thought experiment – think of someone two cubicles, two doors, two workstations over. How is your work connected to that person's work? How does that person's work support your work, and vice versa? Now think about the person ten doors down, three floors up, or six area codes away. What is the system that connects you? Now walk down two cubicles, doors, etc., and ask that person the same question. Are you complementary parts of a system, or only marbles rattling around the same box?

*The right players are not necessarily the best players. You're not looking for the most competent, you're looking for those who want to be part of a team environment.*

Antonio Soave, Former Kansas Secretary of Commerce,

Chairman and CEO of Capistrano Global Advisory Services, former head coach at Ave Maria University in Florida and Franciscan University of Steubenville in Ohio, and former semi-professional player

A system is different from a collection of top performers or staff who show up at the same meetings. A system is the way in which people work together to accomplish the organization's goal or achieve the task at hand. There are lots of systems to accomplish lots of things – all may share elements (research and development, marketing, sales) but the weight put on each can vary based on the need and the staff available to meet the need. Do you like people to "stay in their lanes" so they can focus on what they're best at, or do you prefer "radical collaboration" in which everyone is swerving all over the road? Do you want a flat organization or is a tight hierarchy best for the task at hand?

You also need the people in the system. Your system needs to reflect the staffing realities of the moment. Most managers do not have the luxury of looking at the goal that needs to be accomplished, designing the best system to achieve that goal, and then hiring the best possible talent to fit the needed roles. Managers inherit staff and have limited hiring and firing ability for a range of reasons including corporate culture, contracts, fear of lawsuits, and so forth. Most companies, like most professional soccer teams, also have financial constraints. No company can remain profitable and not pay attention to salaries.

*In an operating room, everyone needs to work together to ensure the patient's safety. Everyone needs to know why their task is important, what everyone else is doing and why what others are doing is important, and how to adjust if necessary. This is a universal metaphor ... You have to explain the system to make sure everyone is invested, that everyone has an important role.*
Sonia Ruiz-Bolanos, Councilmember Gerson Lehrman

Group, former Managing Director of Johns Hopkins Medicine International, former intermural and rec league player

Most companies, like Athletic de Bilbao, have regional constraints as well – you may persuade a CEO or other senior executive to move for a job, but it can be tough to persuade middle and lower level staff to do so. Most managers have to mix designing the ideal system with ensuring their system fits the staff they both have and those they can reasonably hire and fire. A good manager designs a system based on the staff he has and the system that will best accomplish the goal. It does no good to imagine the perfect system but not have the staff to successfully work in that system, and it is similarly unwise to accept the staff one has in the roles they are performing and leave them alone in the hopes that they accomplish your goals. As a manager you need to imagine the ideal and work within reality to achieve it; you need to think about short-term and long-term strategy, as well as immediate and future tactics, all at the same time.

Middle managers are often in tough spots because they have less control over the system in which their staff works and less control over who is on their staff. They need to constantly think about ways to make formal or informal adjustments to the system and to those who are on the team. This can mean reassigning tasks or creating formal or informal groups to accomplish certain goals.

> ... *great coaches and great business leaders know how to adapt their 'system' (the dynamics of the players you have) to get the most out of the individuals and accomplish the goals of the [organization] ... this also pertains to their knowledge of individuals' strengths and weaknesses and adapting the system to exploit the strengths and cover the weaknesses*

Alan Dietrich, Chief Operating Officer Sporting KC

Many managers find they are more like rec league team captains than coaches of Barcelona, Arsenal, or DC United. Someone without a formal title or position may be put in charge of a project, or put in a group tasked with achieving a goal, and find that she is in charge of keeping the group on task. In this case there is almost no leeway to hire or fire and all of the power is in creating the system. The best of these managers do what the best CEOs do – figure out the best system that accounts for the talent in the room. It does little good to design a system without accounting for the abilities of those in the group to fill the roles, and it is equally folly to coast along and hope the group succeeds. The most successful managers in these roles look at the goal or task at hand, look at the strengths and weaknesses of those asked to achieve the goal, and build systems that merge the two.

This is a role that is familiar to most consultants. A consultant is often brought in to complete a specific task or accomplish a specific goal (launch a product for example). That consultant has to work with the team already in place at the organization that hired him. The consultant may be able to supplement that team with other consultants or contractors as needed (within financial constraints, subject to the veto of the client and accounting for the client's favorite writer, least favorite public opinion researcher, and nephew). The consultant has to look at the task, look at the staff already in place, look at what new staff she can bring on, and set up the best system under the circumstances.

*Success on a project or a consulting team requires not just knowing what I need to do, but what others are doing as well. You have to make sure you have the right people in the right roles and that everyone shares the same vision.*
Ken Alexander, Manager at a large consulting firm and former professional player

Whatever system you have, stick to it when things are going well and when things are going poorly. In the face of a crisis it is tempting to do the most expedient thing rather than rely on the system to respond. Managers will get out ahead of their staff or disrupt expected chains of command or communication. Junior staff will see confusion and either freelance or do nothing at all. If top management is seen to be working outside the system they are supposed to be enforcing, middle management and junior staff will either follow or do nothing – neither of which is helpful. An important point of a system is to be able to absorb shocks or attacks, but it can only do so if the system remains intact. When given bad news the worst thing a manager can do is circumvent the system that has been set up to deal with things like bad news. The system should be allowed to respond to the problem. If part of the problem was the system, then the system should be changed, but deliberately and with full communication of what is expected of everyone.

Just as soccer teams abandon (or drift away from) systems when they are winning, so can companies. Companies that are doing well can get lazy. Managers can come to believe that they are responsible for the success of the business and begin to act as if they are apart from, or above, the system that makes the organization go. And pretty soon, the organization can falter and lose ground to a more disciplined competitor.

A number of years ago I was hired to run a campaign for a national trade association to prevent changes to the federal tax code. Given the constraints posed by time and money, and the team with which I had to work, I designed a targeted campaign that set up some national messaging around the public support for the industry and then made the case for the industry to a handful of elected officials in their home states or districts. The trade association had some good case studies of their impact in a few regions, had a good young and underutilized employee who was expert in social media, and coincidentally the association had some good reports scheduled to come out. I hired a public opinion researcher to inform the effort. I pushed hard for a strong social media effort to take advantage of the expertise and time of the young staff member, and did media outreach around the results of the public opinion research. We avoided the temptation to do attention-getting stunts or marches, did not fly in industry executives from around the country, make TV ads, or engage in many of the other traditional tactics of a campaign. We developed a plan based on who we had and what we could afford. I ensured the system was collaborative, with the lobbyists and association staff and my team in as many meetings together as possible so they could all hear what the others were doing and offer ideas. The system relied on constant feedback and as much focus as possible. I could have used the entire budget on lobbyists and run a parallel effort to what the association was already doing. I could have just done national press, could have taken out newspaper ads, could have done any number of other things. These would have used up the limited resources, been focused, and would not have taken as much time from the trade association. Those approaches would also have not taken advantage of the talent I had at hand, the players already on the team. In the end, the tax provisions were kept intact and the industry is thriving.

*You need to know what skill you bring to the team and how that fits in the system. The same is true in a company: what skill do you bring? How does it fit?*
Lori Lindsey, former US Women's National Team midfielder, soccer trainer, human rights advocate

As a manager and an employee you need to know your role in the system and you need to stick to that role. You need to focus on your assigned task, work with the larger group to make the collective assignment work, and you need to keep your eyes open to cover for your colleagues in the system when needed. Rather than think from your job out to the greater whole, think about the organizational or unit goal back to your role and ensure you are working that larger system.

## Locker Room Notes for Managers

Have a system. You aren't just hiring and managing staff, you are constructing a system of people to advance your goal. As you build your system think about who you have already and what their strengths and weaknesses are and the opportunities for hiring and constraints on firing you face. Then build the best system for the challenge at hand with an eye to the ideal system you want to build in the future.

Look at your staff and build a system that takes advantages of their strengths and weaknesses as you keep an eye on the system you want and the people you want in those roles.

If you are in an ad hoc system, or there is no one providing clear direction, you should slot into where your best role is, while also talking to those around you about which system works best for the task at hand. This conversation may lead to your being put in charge, in which case think again about the system and staff you have to work with.

## Locker Room Notes for Staff

Know that you are part of a system, and know what that part is. If you are not sure about the system or your role, ask.

If you are in an ad hoc system, or there is no one providing clear direction, you should slot into where your best role is, while also talking to those around you about which system works best for the task at hand. This conversation may lead to your being put in charge, in which case think again about the system and staff you have to work with.

## Endnotes

1.  Most professional games only allow three substitutions per

team during a game, and once a player is substituted he or she cannot go back into the game. If you use all three substitutions and someone gets hurt with 15 minutes to play your team plays a person short for 15 minutes, and if you take someone out in the 30th minute you can't put them back in. Most rec leagues allow unlimited substitutions, players come and go with few restrictions, in part to ensure everyone gets to play and in part to minimize the risk of injury.

2.  There are serious amateur sides that have tryouts and formal practices and such but most local leagues are of the local duffer variety.

3.  Pickup soccer games can have as few or many players a side as show up. There is a regular Saturday morning game in my neighborhood that on a nice morning can have two simultaneous, side-by-side games of 9v9 and sometimes a third of 4v4, all in a pretty confined space, and on a cold morning or holiday weekend only one game of 5v5. In each case players sort out where they are needed and go there.

# Chapter 4

# Soccer Fields Are Loud

Soccer players constantly talk and listen. On the field they coach and are coached by each other, warn each other of threats, and point out opportunities. The best organizations are the same. The best staff constantly talk to each other, listen to each other, and trust each other.

*Smart soccer players ... feed their teammates a concise stream of information that helps those teammates solve their soccer problems. Note for coaches: Demand useful communication from your players in every possible exercise. It's amazing how much easier soccer is when players are giving and receiving useful information.*
Dan Blank Soccer IQ: Things That Smart Players Do

*Even when your roles are clear, there will be things that are ambiguous and you need to communicate. ("I got it!" "All you ...") I was thinking about an area on our staff where we have two people whose roles are clear, but there's always stuff that's a little murky – and I thought about how when like you have a center-mid and a wing midfielder and a ball comes in-between them, no matter how clear the roles are they just need to talk to decide who's taking it.*
Jerry Hauser, CEO, The Management Center and and lifelong mediocre pickup player

Soccer games are loud. Stadiums are often designed to ensure the noise is trapped and echoed – making them even louder. Soccer fans are famous for their banners, songs, and chants. Take away the fans and the game is still loud – players talk constantly, telling their colleagues what is going on around them and helping them figure out what to do next.

Soccer is also a constant reminder of our cognitive limits. The field is big and there is a lot going on. No one person can see all of it – and even if one player could see everything, the game happens too quickly and there is no way to process all the options fast enough without help. Soccer players therefore rely on systems solutions, a network of decision makers and option providers to make sense of the complex and quickly changing environment and to inform the best decision.

> *Players have odd instincts on the field. They often shout your name when they want the ball. I know my name. What I may not know in a given situation, especially if under duress, is where you are. So what I need to know right then is what I don't already know. Tell me where you want the ball or where you are – the sort of run you're making or the kind of pass you want played – and how much time I have to play it. Because maybe I can't see the guy coming in from behind about to clean me out. Where and when. That's it. In compressed time and space, give me the vital information.*
> Brian Straus, Sports Illustrated Writer, former player and youth coach

This is why defenders tell each other to force an opponent wide or to cover a forward streaking down the field; defenders tell midfielders or forwards they are running past them or to send a ball down the line; forwards tell midfielders with the ball that an opponent is coming up on him or her. Goalkeepers yell at everybody. This chatter serves as ongoing instruction from everyone to everyone. Players let each other know when they see trouble coming and ask for support, they let each other know about unseen threats, tell them when they have support, and alert them to opportunities. This collective instruction improves the actions of individuals and makes it more likely the system will succeed.

Good input is specific, immediate, and actionable. For

example, if a defender is facing someone faster than he is, everyone knows it (the defender most acutely). "Run faster" is terrible advice to the defender – if he could run faster he wouldn't need the help. "Cut the angle" is good advice, as is "back off two steps I'll cover" or even "switch sides, the other forward isn't as quick." Other examples include "defend him better" (bad) versus "force him left, he hates his left" (good), "pass it to me better" (bad), "put the ball over my head, I'll chase it" (good), "stop giving the ball away" (bad), and "if you're not sure, knock the ball up field or out" (good).

In addition to offering instruction and providing information in the moment, players encourage each other when a teammate makes a mistake – "unlucky" is heard more often on a soccer field than anywhere else outside of a casino. Even if the failure wasn't about luck but rather a poor decision or poor execution, teammates will often encourage rather than scold. As a teammate on a rec league team on which I played noted, people know when they have made a mistake – you don't have to tell them (though I once had a coach who said "bad luck" is English for "you suck"). Soccer players also berate each other for not being in the right place, for missing an obvious option, or for being lazy. The yelling isn't about the quality of the person or the purity of that person's motives. The yelling is about specific actions and behaviors.

Players also talk to each other during lulls or when the play is on another part of the field to share information and make adjustments during the game. Defenders routinely huddle to talk about how to adjust to attackers, who should cover where, and where to move with the ball. Forwards talk to each other about where to move, where to look for a pass, and how to beat defenders. Players also ask questions – "where do you want the ball?" "how do you want to handle it when they switch?" These on-the-fly conversations do not compensate for larger strategic conversations that happen before the game or at half time, but these minor adjustments can make the difference between success and failure.

> *In soccer, the key to being successful as a team is talking to your teammates on the field during games. Good communication habits can make the difference between a good team and a great one. Teams that communicate well commit fewer errors, make better passes, and are prepared for defenders marking them from behind ...*
>
> *On the other hand, a lack of communication often results in coverage mistakes and getting caught off-guard. It also becomes harder to string passes together and maintain possession, especially in the midfield. If your team is underperforming, it's likely that a little work on communication could be the remedy.*

How to Communicate on the Soccer Field

One weekend morning I watched two small-sided games happening at the same time on adjacent fields. Both games had skilled players and were fun to watch. The notable difference between the games was that one team in one game was doing all the right things, but not talking about them. Players were making terrific runs, getting open, creating space, and otherwise moving well as a team. But the players weren't talking to each other – no one making a run shouted for the ball, no one behind the person with the ball made suggestions about where to pass or what to do next. As a result the team spent most of the time defending and predictably was losing. Soccer skills are a necessary, but not sufficient, element of success. In the other game, the team that was winning was doing all the right things and communicating constantly. The players knew what they were doing, and because of all of the communication they knew what everyone else was doing as well and therefore how to respond to the unfolding action.

The corollary to talking is listening. Players listen not just for warnings or options, but for input and direction. They need to gather information about the play in the moment and about their actions throughout the game. Players gather information about unseen opportunities and potential threats, and how to adjust and respond. They know that the best advice is given to help the team win, not to aggrandize or undermine a player or play.

Players also know that if they don't listen, their teammates will start to ignore them. If someone never responds to a call to pass the ball, doesn't listen to an impending threat, or go cover someone when told, that player will soon find himself out of the game. Teammates will be reluctant to pass him the ball and will shift to cover assumed defensive lapses. Players who don't listen quickly find themselves without teammates or a team at all.

One Saturday morning I was playing pickup in my usual outside back role and a midfielder on my team who had come back to help on defense was trapped with the ball deep in our own end. I ran around behind the player with the ball, shouted "heel" (as in "kick the ball backwards with your heel" not "stop chasing that squirrel") and without looking he rolled the ball backwards toward the sound of my voice. I received the ball and passed to a waiting teammate in one motion. The immediate threat against us was resolved and we created a threat going the other way. This worked because the midfielder saw the need to support the defense, another teammate put himself in a position to help, and I saw a way to bridge the problem and solution. The midfielder did not stand in the center of the field waiting for the defense to put out the threat or give up a goal, he came back to help, and I did not sit and wait for him to get out a jam, I went over to help solve it.[1] The three of us worked as a little unit turning the problem into an opportunity. No one worried about titles or roles, they just did what the situation demanded. We were a small system embedded in a larger system working toward a shared goal.

Talking and listening only work if there is trust. Those doing the talking have to trust the person they are talking to is listening and can do as asked. Those listening have to trust that the information is accurate and actionable.

Talking and listening are part of an ongoing conversation about how to maximize resources, minimize weaknesses, and advance a shared goal. As a player I need to trust that the person I'm talking to shares my goal of winning the game, even if it means he gets a little less glory. I also need to trust that the person talking to me isn't setting me up for failure, and takes into account both my strengths and weaknesses. As a player, I need to know that my teammates have my back, both literally and figuratively. If I don't trust that the other ten players on my team are fully with me I will be afraid to take risks, I will make mistakes, and the team will suffer. Similarly, if my teammates do not trust that I am listening they will stop talking and stop involving me in the game at all, thereby weakening the overall effort and damaging the chances for success.

Organizations and the fields they are in – manufacturing, retail, non-profits, whatever – are complex systems that are always changing, and it seems the rate of change is accelerating. No one person can see or process all of the information fast enough to respond. As such everyone inside an organization needs to constantly coach and be coached. And they must trust each other.

This chatter is expected on soccer fields, but in the workplace it can be frowned on. People may be afraid to offer advice to peers or superiors, or reluctant to share information either because information is viewed as power or because those who receive the information may not want to hear it. Organizational goals, or goals of individual units, may not be clear or shared. Managers might reward individual performance, even if that performance comes at the expense of the success of the larger team.

Soccer teams made up of good, but not great, players who work together as a team often beat teams made up of stars who do not work together. Similarly, organizations comprised up of good (but not great) staff can out-perform and out-earn competitors made up of star performers who work for themselves or their divisions rather than for the organization as a whole. The best employees at all levels seek input from peers, superiors, and those who work for them. They ask questions and take the answers seriously. The questions these top performers ask in the office are the same ones soccer players ask on the field – what threats am I missing? Who is about to beat me to the sale and how can I use my strengths to get there first? What opportunities am I missing and how can I get others involved to advance the organization's goals? What information do I need right now? What are my options in the moment, and how can I adjust my behavior to increase the chances for team success?

The best offices are full of people seeking and offering advice on how to advance the organization's mission.

*It turns out that the best way to improve performance and minimize risk isn't to tightly manage [call center] reps, but instead liberate them to engage with one another and share both best practices and lessons learned in handling customer service requests.*
Lara Ponomareff, Lauren Pragoff, and Matthew Dixon "Let Your Call Center Reps Collaborate"

Good employees talk. They let each other know about opportunities, offer support, and point out opportunities and threats that might be missed. This talk includes instructions on the fly, leads for the sales teams, and ideas for marketing. This talk also includes input about ongoing projects and navigating ongoing challenges. The best colleagues are always helping each other succeed by letting them know that a person for whom a presentation is being prepared tends to generally be agreeable early then micromanage very late in the process, or that a VP wants to hear arguments both for and against an idea before proceeding.

Because this sort of talk may not be as expected at an office as it is on a field, managers and staff may need to solicit it and make talk the norm. For example, after a meeting a manager could pull aside someone with whom she doesn't regularly interact and ask "what's the key takeaway you got? How can my division help you achieve that goal?" Before a presentation a manager can ask another manager "when you presented to this group what did you see? What do I need to watch out for?" You can stop people in the hall and ask for their take on the organization that day, ask for ideas for new markets or product improvements. Staff at all levels can engage everyone at the organization in conversations about making the organization better.

To help create a culture of conversation, managers can ask fellow directors (or vice presidents or associates or whatever) what she is hearing about threats and opportunities and ask what advice she is getting from her teams. Staff can create an expectation of coaching and being coached.

The Chairman of the Board of Directors when I was a Vice President at the US Institute of Peace was Stephen J. Hadley. Steve served as the National Security Advisor for President George W. Bush and is among the most respected national security experts out there. He was also a terrific colleague. One of his habits was to ask people what they thought of an event or meeting, without regard to the person's role or title. If you were in the elevator with Steve after a meeting you were both in, you could expect to be asked for your opinion. He did not ask lightly or to pass time, he asked because he wanted to know so that he could improve next time. As a result Steve kept getting better, the staff wanted to do more for him and the organization because he valued their input, and USIP kept improving as an institution. Steve is not a soccer fan, but this is exactly the sort of behavior in which top players engage.

*Swarm intelligence, which brings to mind the image of a hive of bees working together, requires people to gather information independently, process and combine it in social interactions, and use it to solve cognitive problems, according to behavioral biologist Jens Krause. It has an advantage over other systems in that individuals get the opportunity to lead the swarm and affect what it does. Moreover, because people act collectively, they can consider more factors, come up with more solutions, and make better decisions.*

Wolfgang Jenewein, Thomas Kochanek, Marcus Heidbrink and Christian Schimmelpfennig, "Learning Collaboration from Tiki-Taka Soccer"

You cannot take all the advice just as you cannot pass the ball to everyone who is calling for it. And at some point you will be beaten by those who are better and you have to accept the setback and find other ways to succeed. But if you establish an environment in which giving and taking input is expected, people will give and take input, and the organization will be more likely to succeed.

When you get good advice, take it. If you hear a good idea, go with it. Thank those who give you advice, regardless of the advice's quality, to encourage more of it. Create a culture of listening as well as of talking.

*... comedian-turned-Minnesota senator [Al Franken] acknowledges the "fine line between showing up a jerk and being one myself" at Senate hearings, citing a time when he badgered "a guy named Tevi Troy from the Hudson Institute, a right-wing think tank in Washington."...There was laughter in the room as the witness squirmed, but my health care staffer, Hannah Katch, quickly pushed a note in front of me: 'You're being an a — hole,' ... after the hearing he praised Katch to his staff and instructed them to let him know when he was being a jerk.*

Politico

All of this can only work if you and your colleague trust each other. You have to know that you have each other's backs, and that you will only succeed or fail as a team. This means not only not lying ("did I say the VP loves lots of slides with densely packed information? I meant to say the VP hates slides and would prefer to just discuss the idea based on a one page memo, sorry about that. Can I have your office?"); it also means sharing information that can help others succeed. Become a good source of good information, not someone who hoards information. If you look out for your colleagues' best interests and for your shared goals you and your colleagues will succeed together.

Organizations, like soccer teams, have people with big egos and personal agendas. If you trust each other, and trust that by working together everyone will be seen to be higher performers and more successful, then the individual egos get fed as a result of a team trusting each other and working together.

## Locker Room Notes for Managers

Ask for specific input – i.e., "what would have been a better example in that presentation?" – and general input, i.e., "what am I missing?" Take, and be seen to have taken, that input to help create a culture of coaching. Follow up with a staffer you talk to, thank her for the input, and explain either why you didn't take it or what happened when you did. Tell that staffer's immediate supervisor and let the supervisor know you think more highly of him for having staff willing to honestly give good input.

Publicly call out people who gave you good input.

## Locker Room Notes for Staff

Ask for input and take it.

Be, and be seen to be, eager to learn and improve.

When asked, give honest input:

When the input is ignored, don't take it personally – the input is needed for the same reason it might not be taken; there is more

48

Soccer Fields Are Loud

going on that you can see.

When the input is taken do not take credit or change your behavior; giving input is like showing up on time and making fresh coffee when the pot is empty – it's just part of your job.

## Endnotes

1. Pickup soccer is its own fascinating culture. No matter where in the world you are, or what time of day or night you want to play, you can find a game if you look hard enough. The games with which I am most familiar have a regular core of people with roughly the same skill level who all meet at the same place and same time every week. Some groups chip in and buy miniature goals that fold up, some have cones. Many use what's around – gym bags, shoes, garbage cans, one former professional told me he and his friends would move headstones in an abandoned graveyard to mark goals. Sometime there are actual goals if you're lucky enough to play on a real field. Visiting players can jump in the game if there is enough room and if the group invites them (most do). Pickup etiquette requires you bring a dark shirt and light shirt (no gray) and go where needed to make the teams even. A terrific book on the topic is *Finding the Game* by Gwendolyn Oxenham who was a serious player in college. She and her then-boyfriend (who was also a serious college player) traveled the world playing pickup everywhere from a London park, to a prison in Bolivia, to Kenya with moonshine brewers. The book was turned into a documentary called *Pelada,* which is good, but not as good as the book.

## Chapter 5

# Know When to Run, When to Walk, and When to Rest

Soccer players know that recovery time between sprints is critical to success over the course of a 90-minute game. The best managers and staff also know the importance of taking time to recover so they can be as effective as possible when needed most.

*Sometimes (soccer) is a game of speed and sometimes it's a game of stamina. There are times when you need to sprint, times when you should walk or trot to save energy for that next sprint, and times when you need to keep pace to stay with the play for that moment when you become a key part of the attack; the need for varying speed, knowing when to exert energy and when to reserve energy. The need for varying speed, knowing when to exert energy and when to reserve energy and that constant give-take is a much needed skill-set in management and business.*
Ashley Starks Amin, former NCAA Division I player at The George Washington University, social entrepreneur

*R and R (rest and relaxation) is very important. You have to find time to goof around and let off steam. One of my rules [at the Embassy] was I wasn't clocking hours the staff were at their desks. No one worked weekends – over six years, my staff only worked weekends once. The counter is that if I ping you at 3am you need to be responsive. If I ping you at 3am it is because we have a problem, not because I want you to remind me of something in the morning.*
Ambassador Arturo Sarukhan, Mexican Ambassador to the United States 2007–2013

Soccer is physically demanding. Fields are usually longer and wider than football fields, each half is 45 minutes long, there are no timeouts, and each team is allowed only three substitutions a game. It is not surprising that anyone watching the game quickly sees that a lot of players spend a lot of time standing around or casually jogging from one place to the next.

Professional soccer players cover six or seven miles during a typical game. In a 2014 World Cup game against Ghana. US midfielder Michael Bradley ran 7.9 miles and defender Geoff Cameron 6.4, the most and least of the US starters that day, excluding goalkeeper Tim Howard who ran 2.9 miles. Not all these miles are run at once, and not all at the same speed. Defenders sprint 70 or 80 yards up the field to support an attack and sprint back just as far and just as quickly to defend, central midfielders regularly sprint 20 or 30 yards side to side and up and back, and forwards make 60 yard sprints to catch up to passes. Rec league soccer tends to allow unlimited substitutions, the fields are often smaller than professional fields, and the halves sometimes shorter, so there is even less running (in defense of rec league soccer players, most of us do not get paid to be physically fit so a bit of leeway seems fair; we are just as winded as the pros after a game because we have less wind to lose).

Soccer is about being able to use short bursts of energy when needed and knowing when to rest and let your body recover in time for the next burst. Players who try to sprint for 90 minutes fade physically and mentally and become liabilities to their team. Players who never sprint or push themselves are not contributing to the team's success as much as they should.

Soccer players have to pace themselves so they are sharp both physically and mentally when that sharpness is needed most. The physical challenge of sprinting for 90 minutes is obvious – and I can attest that the older one gets the more obvious it becomes. If a defender has made a run up the field to support the attack but doesn't have the energy to come back on defense it could end up costing his team a goal.

Mental fitness is at least as important as physical fitness. Tired players make silly mistakes. Their brains cannot keep up with the speed of the play and as a result they can get caught out of position, their passes go astray, and they can commit silly fouls. Soccer players cannot stumble their way through 90 minutes, they need to be as mentally sharp at the end of the game as they are at the beginning.

> *When you run, you run. When you walk, you walk. It's about pacing yourself. You need to have the judgement to know when to go full speed or lay off. Leadership on the field or in the board room requires that you know about how to sense rhythms and understand timing.*
>
> Neil Richardson, Founder Emergent Action, co-author of *Preparing for a World that Doesn't Exist – Yet*, former professional soccer player Richmond Kickers

Successful pacing requires making judgments about when to run forward to support the attack or run back to help defend, when to move to space to create options, and when to run to cover space left by a teammate. It also means knowing when not to run, which opportunities are least likely to materialize, which plays may break down before you can help, and which teammates are already moving so you don't have to. When not running you have to know whether to walk, jog, or stand still. As an outside back I tend to make runs up the field when it looks like outside support can help, when it looks like we will keep the ball in the opponent's end for a few passes, and when there is enough support at the back in case I get caught out of position. If a central defender goes up into the attack or to be an extra body on a corner kick, I walk over from my position on the right or left to a position in the middle. I casually slide into the gap, saving my energy for the next attack and supporting a teammate with more energy. If the midfielder in front of me is catching his breath I'll run past him and tell him to hang back for a minute. Not all decisions are the right ones, defenders get caught out of position all the time and attacks fizzle out because not enough players are running up in support, but these mistakes and missed opportunities are better than a group of players guaranteed to make mistakes and miss opportunities no matter how good because they are exhausted.

Good players also know that the ball moves faster than they can run and they know the ball never gets tired, so they "let the ball do the work." The day after a game is typically a day off, and professional coaches regularly give players a few days at a time during the season to let the mind and body recover. Unlike most jobs, there is an offseason in soccer during which players take time away from the game and their teammates so their bodies can recover and they can regain their focus. While rec leagues run year round, each "season" only lasts a few months and most of us take a few weeks or months off between seasons – even if we play pickup when our league is on a break the pressure is off.

But a lot of people think they should sprint all the time when they are at work. In spite of the bottomless well of research finding non-stop work is as counterproductive as non-stop sprinting, many of us continue to work well past the point of fatigue. The results are the same at work as they are on the field: decisions made while tired are often flawed, actions taken while tired are often poor.

*... a Senior Manager ... described to me how, by using local clients, telecommuting, and controlling information about his whereabouts, he found ways to work and travel less, without being found out. He told me: 'I skied five days last week. I took calls in the morning and in the evening but I was able to be there for my son when he needed me to be, and I was able to ski five days in a row.' He clarified that these were work days, not vacation days: 'No, no one knows where I am ... Those boundaries are only practical with my local client*

*base ... Especially because we're mobile, there are no boundaries.'*
*Despite his deviance from the ideal worker expectation, however,*
*senior colleagues viewed him as a star; indeed, one Partner*
*described him to me as a 'rising star,' who worked 'much harder*
*than' he himself did. This assessment — in combination with Lloyd's*
*top performance rating and his promotion to Partner that year —*
*suggests he had successfully passed in the eyes of senior members*
*of the firm as an ideal worker.*
Erin Reid, "Why Some Men Pretend to Work 80-Hour Weeks"

I live and work in Washington, D.C., a city in which people brag about the endless hours they put in at the office. The assumption is that the amount of time one spends at the office is evidence of how important one is; busyness is a marker of social status and importance. There is an implied inverse relationship between the time someone's phone is off and their importance to their firm and the nation as a whole. Washington is not unique – you hear phrases like "markets never sleep" and I once knew a copyright attorney in New York who routinely slept in his office. There is a cultural urge to always be seen to be working.

It is also true that a lot of what passes for work, isn't. People lie about how much time they are at work, and a lot of time "at work" is spent online, chatting, or otherwise not actually working. One bestseller claims you can have a four-hour work week by increasing your efficiency and outsourcing as much as possible (assuming you have the sort of job that doesn't require you to actually be at your job – a luxury most people don't have).

Hours spent at a desk or on a phone are poor proxies for how much time one spends being productive – and worse can make one's work worse. The more hours you put in, the more likely you are to have to put in even more hours correcting the mistakes you made while you were working too much. Your brain at the office is just like your brain on the soccer field – it can only do so much before it starts to run down and you start to make mistakes, mistakes you have to take time to correct later – or time others will have to take to fix your mistakes. Either way, it is time that could be better spent doing almost anything else (like resting). And as in soccer, work takes a physical toll. The health risks of spending too much time at the office are well documented. Our bodies were no more designed to spend 80 hours a week at the office than they were designed to sprint for 90 minutes.

Professionals in offices should do as professional athletes do: sprint when needed, walk or jog when you can, take days off, and take real vacations.

There are times when you need to work 80 hour weeks and weekends and miss family events and all of that – but those should be bursts, and bursts by definition are temporary. Working at top speed and top focus is unsustainable, and things that are unsustainable stop. This means picking your moments, deciding when you need to put in the extra effort because that effort is more likely than not to advance organizational goals, and it means deciding when to take a pass and let others do the work and get the glory. You do not need to be on every project; in fact being on every project is probably counterproductive. You do not need to be in every pitch meeting or every meeting in the office; let others do the work or let the work happen around you. You need to miss some work so that when you are needed you are at your best. If there is a sales opportunity or technical challenge to which you can add unique or important value and you are not at your sharpest because you exhausted yourself doing unnecessary tasks, you are letting everyone down.

This is easier to do on a soccer field than it is an office, and it is easier said than done. Junior staff at offices can feel intense pressure to the be the first one in and the last one out, middle managers want to show senior managers they deserve the next step up, and senior managers want to continue to demonstrate their value (and feed their egos). Men and women face different challenges, with more pressure on women to "lean in" and not be seen as more devoted to their families than their jobs. People get promoted for being seen as "go getters" and are punished for choosing to pass on opportunities.

Congressional offices tend to have a lot of interns during the summer and during the school year, but very few during the break between the end of the spring term and start of summer vacation. Offices have the most interns during the summer, but that also tends to be the slowest time of year in Washington. I worked in an office in which an enterprising intern was around during the few weeks before the summer hordes arrived, and since he was one of the few interns around, he was given a lot of responsibility. The office soon filled with interns, far more than could realistically be put to work, so a lot of them just sat around. The enterprising intern figured out if he was seen sitting around staff would assume he was lazy, but if no one saw him everyone would assume he was off doing something productive for someone else. So he would come to the office in the morning, check with staff to see if there was anything that needed doing, and if not he would go to the movies, see the monuments, or otherwise make himself scarce. The intern would pop back in, check to see if there was work that needed doing, and if not take off again (never telling anyone where he was going of course). At the end of the summer he was the only intern to be offered a job.

Take short breaks during the day. Walk out to get a cup of coffee, with the walk being more important than the beverage. Take a few minutes off to check the soccer scores or just stretch – you don't need to go full Costanza[1], but breaks here and there can have real benefits.

You should take your weekends off. In order to be as effective as possible your brain and body need the time to think about something other than your job. You need to take walks, read, play soccer, watch soccer, talk about soccer, do something that's not your job. And of course you should take vacations. Think of a few weeks off as the off-season; your office will have you back and needs you healthy, refreshed, and energized.

> *Downtime replenishes the brain's stores of attention and motivation, encourages productivity and creativity, and is essential to both achieve our highest levels of performance and simply form stable memories in everyday life.*
>
> Ferris Jabr, "Your Brain Needs More Downtime Than You Think"

It can be extremely difficult to buck this trend, especially for junior staff (millennials already have a reputation of being lazy and entitled, so any move by a 20-something to limit hours could feed an existing stereotype, fairly or otherwise). Managers should model good behavior. They should not regularly email their staff before seven or eight in the morning and not after seven or eight at night, and should avoid emailing over the weekend except in emergencies. Managers should send people home, take them off projects, and kick them out of meetings – and then reward those staff who work hard at work but not at all when not at work. Managers need to model, and be seen to be modelling good behavior. It does no good to tell others to go home while you stay or to tell them not to email while you email. Your actions will speak far louder than your words.

## Locker Room Notes for Managers

Tell your staff to manage their time and energy.

Pull staff off projects that don't need them.

If staff are just sitting around send them home without punishment.

Model good behavior – take the time you need and be seen to be taking the time. Enforce email blackout times. Do not reply to email outside of reasonable hours such as 8 p.m. to 7 a.m. Eventually your staff will catch on and not send you information then.

Do not do things that appear to be busy but that do not advance the team goals – do not mistake motion for progress.

## Locker Room Notes for Staff

When you are at work, work. Do not just hang around and complain about how much you are working, or do things that appear to be busy but that do not advance the team goals – do not mistake motion for progress.

Make an agreement with your manager that you will not check email outside of set hours such as 8 p.m. to 7 a.m.

## Endnotes

1.   In a Seinfeld episode called "The Nap" George Costanza has a mattress built into his desk so he can nap.

# Chapter 6

# Where the Ball Isn't

A lot of soccer is about where the ball might be next. Players create options when their team has the ball, anticipate what the other team wants to do, and move to create options and minimize threats. The best managers and staff do the same. They see where they might be useful to help a project succeed or to prevent negative effects of actions, and move to those areas. The best staff and managers anticipate and respond.

*In football, the worst blindness is only seeing the ball.*
Attributed to Brazilian playwright, journalist, and novelist Nelson Falcão Rodrigues

*Leaders are creators of opportunity for others.*
Bill Treasurer, "Leaders Create Opportunity"

A lot of soccer is about where the ball isn't.

Soccer fields are typically between 110–120 yards long and between 70–80 yards wide.[1] The ball is about 24 inches in diameter and at most there are 22 players and one referee on the field at a time. That's a lot of space to fill and not a lot of stuff to fill it.

Anyone who has seen little kids play soccer is familiar with the cluster approach to the game: there is a mass of children, a ball pops out, children mass around the ball, the ball pops out, and the process repeats. These kids think in individual units – "I see the ball. I must kick the ball." Skilled players understand the game as a system in which 11 people work together to get the ball into the net while preventing the opposing 11 people from doing the same. This abstract conception of the game moves it from hordes of people acting individually and uni-directionally to a system that acts as a whole and multi-directionally. Players far from the ball will move in ways or to spaces that advance the team's goal to score and prevent the opposition from scoring. They work as part of a system rather than as individuals.

The best players play best not just when they have the ball, but also when they don't. Soccer commentators talk about a player's movement away from where the ball is to create space or support the team. In soccer-speak, the best players work just as hard off the ball as they do on the ball.

Somewhat unbelievably given her performance in the 2015 World Cup finals, American Star and FIFA Women's Player of the Year in 2015, Carly Lloyd, was cut from the US national team early in her career because she did not work hard enough when she did not have the ball at her feet. Lloyd needed to become a "two-way player" to succeed. She met the challenge, regained her place on the team and became a star who worked for her teammates and was named the best in the world 2015.

*A smart player is constantly asking herself, 'what if?' and 'what's next?'*
Dan Blank Soccer IQ: Things That Smart Players Do

Part of working hard off the ball is covering for teammates on defense and supporting them when they attack. Working off the ball includes anticipating where the ball might go next and getting there first, and also creating space on the field for others to run into. You need to keep track of your own players as well as the opposition's players so that you can act on a decision as soon as the ball is at your feet. If you wait until you receive the ball to think about what to do next, you're toast. You need to anticipate what the opposition is about to do, where the next pass will go or the direction of the next attack and move to help. If an opposing player has the ball and it is not your job to cover or mark that person, you need to be thinking about where that player wants to pass the ball or where he wants to try to dribble it, and you have to move to cut off the angle, pass, or run, and limit that player's options. Passing the ball is only part of the job; after you pass it you need to put yourself in a position to help again. Good soccer players don't pass and wait, they pass and move.

When your team has the ball you need to think about where you want the ball to be next – or where you want the other team to think it is about to go. In soccer you create options for others by creating space – you put others in a position to succeed by where you run to and where you position yourself. The best players move to where the ball isn't yet, or run toward teammates who are in trouble and offer a passing option or support, or draw opposition players away from the person with the ball. The best players move off the ball not just with the ball.

Countless goals at all levels of the game, from pickup in the park to World Cup finals, are created by players without the ball moving into empty space and creating options for their teammates.

> *The ball turned over in our half, our right back completed a great forward pass to our attacking midfielder just over half field on the right side. Seeing this I started moving towards our opponent's goal but also drifting away from their defenders who were moving towards the ball. My teammate was able to impeccably pick me out with a sublime pass right into my path.*
> Andrew Wenger, professional soccer player describing the setup to first goal he scored for the Philadelphia Union, "Trust Your Instincts...If you can"

The best managers and employees anticipate, support, and create options for others. They position themselves to help before they are called upon to act, and find ways to support the organization's success after their specific task is completed. Part of working as a team rather than as an individual is keeping an eye on how colleagues are working toward the goal, anticipating challenges and pre-emptively addressing them, finding ways to support your colleagues, creating options for them, and following up to keep helping. The best staff and managers are always asking "what if?" and "what next?"

When you are focused on your task, you need to be 100 percent focused on that task. But you shouldn't sit at your desk waiting to be asked to help, and when your task is done you should find ways to help whatever happens next. Work and organizations are made up of discreet units of effort that happen in a specific amount of time. But those discreet units of effort only matter to the extent they are part of a larger string of units that build on each other to advance the goal.

There are two parts to this – responding to immediate needs, and anticipating opportunities. Responding to immediate needs is easy, and what we often think of when we think about working like a team. When your colleagues are swamped, what support do they need? We are used to jumping in when something big happens – maternity leave, illness, family tragedy, and so forth. By definition that support is out of the norm, people take up special responsibilities because of special circumstances. That is why when your colleagues are swamped with a proposal you step in to cover them at meetings. Good colleagues slide into the gaps that emerge through circumstance.

*To be more effective at building relationships with consumers online, companies need a cross-functional social media team, one where marketing works together with other departments. Distributing social responsibilities to relevant people across the organization can be efficient, be effective, and help make one-on-one customer engagement scalable.*
Keith A. Quesenberry, Social Media Is Too Important to Be Left to the Marketing Department

Responding is about reacting to things that go wrong. Anticipation is about preventing bad things from happening to begin with, and helping things that are going right go better. Anticipation can be tougher, but it also is what distinguishes good staff and organizations from great ones.

For example, imagine that you're in the marketing department, and part of the social media team. Viewed one way, marketing's job is to draw attention to events or products. Someone outside of marketing and higher up the food chain declares a big thing is happening, and that the company wants it to get a lot of attention. The head of marketing tells you to make it a big deal in Twitter, Instagram, etc. You take this directive, come up with a plan, and on the appointed date and time push it out. The event ends, you put the task away, and await the next task. If someone in the social media unit of the marketing division is sick, or has a family emergency, you log a few extra hours to cover for them, but you're still the person pushing out tweets.

The most successful organizations need staff who do more than respond. The most successful organizations need staff who think and act like soccer players, staff who anticipate, act, and support. Imagine the same scenario – you do social media for a company, and the social media group reports to the marketing director. Rather than wait for the marketing director's boss to give her an edict, the social media piece of which is passed to you, you could look at the company's goals and set yourself up to support them. If you know the company is expanding its number of retail outlets over the next 24 months, you could adjust your calendar to account for this surge. You could talk to your boss about integrating these openings with the larger marketing effort, internal human resources needs (new outlets mean a need for new staff, which means new onboarding, and so on), public relations and press needs, and customer interaction. You could find ways that social media can support everything before each outlet's opening and help ensure continued success for the outlet after it opens, in addition to the social media push around the opening itself. In this example, you view your role as one of support for the larger organizational goal rather than as just the task at hand. If you are not in the social media group, go ask that group for their ideas and solicit their help – human resources should reach out to the social media folks for help on HR. If you manage the social media group, ask them how they can support the larger marketing efforts, and let your boss(es) know that all of marketing is poised to help the opening of the outlets go well and also to help ensure that everything post-opening is also a success.

Getting from reaction to anticipation can be easier said than done, of course. It takes work to make a shift in thinking and behavior routine (for more on this see the chapter titled "Getting Fit Along the Way"). One way to start getting staff and units to anticipate rather than just respond is to routinely ask how one discreet task can help support other tasks and help those other tasks succeed. For example, a typical feature of many meetings is the reporting in on major projects, upcoming events, victories, and so forth. We've all been in, and all hate, these meetings. They become tedious recitations of other people's self-aggrandizing while participants are left with too little time to talk about shared goals and challenges. One way to change the meeting to make it advance the organizational goal is to ask someone who has just reported how you can help build on their success, or what you can do to ensure that anything left undone or put on the back burner is not forgotten; disrupt the individual-focused flow to offer support that advances the organization's goal and not just the self-promoting goal of the presenter. Find out what the individual is doing and figure out how you can help make that individual effort a system effort, and thus make achieving organizational goals more likely. This is the equivalent of a defender asking a midfielder, "if I get the ball, where do you want me to pass it?" and "after I pass you the ball, I'll run around you on the outside so if you send the ball downfield I'll run and catch up with it, even if you don't get me the ball I will pull a defender with me and give you more space in the middle."

After someone gives a report ask what help that person needs to build on the success, or ask how others can step up to ensure that other priorities get covered. Managers can go a step further by asking others in the meeting for their input, how they could advance the success or if they have capacity to fill in any gaps. A manager can both ask the person doing the reporting where the opportunities and threats are and also ask colleagues to identify them – and step in to build or cover as needed. Before long the manager will not have to ask; those doing the reporting will anticipate the question and make the answers part of the presentation and others will similarly offer ideas and support. Colleagues will see ways to help and offer that help, and they will see gaps and fill the gaps. Importantly, the person doing the asking about opportunities or threats need not be the person with the biggest title at the table, it can be anyone. The point of a system is that everyone works within it. There is a captain or manager to keep order and make sure everyone is playing his or her role, but everyone has to move as a unit.

As in soccer, not all opportunities can be seized – you cannot attempt all of the available passes – and not all potential threats become real. And as in soccer, not all attempts are successful, some passes go astray and some defensive covering does not work. Not every story gets picked up by the press, not every pitch results in a sale, and not every engineering solution works. And that's fine. Individual failure by individuals is part of working as a system, because in a system there is always cover for mistakes.

Smart organizations are always looking for what might happen next. They put themselves to succeed in the future as well as in the present. Where is the industry going? What are your competitors about to do and how can you be in a position to respond (for example, if a competitor is using limited resources to expand into a new market, is their core market now under-serviced and thus a good opportunity for your sales people?). Don't just think about where you are and where your competition is – think about where you, your competition, and industry could be next. Then move there.

Smart managers and staff look for ways to support each other's work. They also keep an eye out for gaps created when others move to seize opportunities and move to fill those gaps.

## Locker Room Notes for Managers

Find ways to support the work of others. Look for ways to make the success of others more successful. Offer ways you can advance the organizational goal.

Offer to help pick up what is not being done while others take advantage of new opportunities.

In meetings ask participants for their ideas about how to advance organizational success or cover potential threats.

Reward staff who find ways to support efforts that advance organizational goals.

## Locker Room Notes for Staff

Find ways to support the work of others. Look for ways to make the success of others more successful. Offer ways you can advance the organizational goal.

Offer to help pick up what is not being done while others take advantage of new opportunities. Offer to file reports, attend meetings, or answer phones. Step in to offer covering support.

## Endnotes

1.  There is no set official length or width of the field in soccer. FIFA, the international governing body of soccer, maintains the official Laws of the Game which prescribe that for international games the field must be between 110–120 yards

long and between 70–80 yards wide. Non-international matches have much more leeway under the Laws, and youth leagues are allowed to make the field smaller.

## Chapter 7

# An Organization Is a Team, Not a Family

Soccer teams are made up of players who come together for the team, but for whom the team is not their life. The best organizations are similarly supportive systems made up of managers and staff who know that while everyone is respected, everyone is also expendable.

*When we go out, we concentrate, we are on the ball and we all speak the same language. Off the pitch, there are a lot of things going on. Everyone has their own habits, their own things to do. You respect that and there's not a lot of talking or guiding people. Everyone is professional enough to cope with situations but on the pitch we want to be a unit from top to bottom.*
Arsenal captain Per Mertesaker, Arsenal Magazine

*Try to imagine disowning your child for poor performance: 'We're sorry Susie, but your mom and I have decided you're just not a good fit. Your table-setting effort has been deteriorating for the past 6 months, and your obsession with ponies just isn't adding any value. We're going to have to let you go. But don't take it the wrong way; it's just family.'*

*Unthinkable, right? But that's essentially what happens when a CEO describes the company as a family, then institutes layoffs. Regardless of what the law says about at-will employment, those employees will feel hurt and betrayed — with real justification.*
Reid Hoffman, Ben Cashnocha, and Chris Yeh "Your Company Is Not a Family"

Players, coaches, and management of soccer teams know they are part of the team to do a job and failure to do that job will result in dismissal. Team members also know that no matter how good they are they can be cut loose if the system changes and the specific skillset of that team member is no longer needed. You have a responsibility to your teammates to do the best you can to advance the goal, but you are expendable. Coaches and captains inspire, push, coax, and encourage their team. Coaches also bench or cut those who fail to live up to expectations, those whose strengths are redundant, whose weaknesses are not compensated for by others on the team, or who are good at what they do but do not fit into the system. Coaches also let players go who want to leave for bigger teams, bigger leagues, more lucrative contracts, or just get a fresh start.

> *Another former (DC United) regular, Chris Pontius, is embracing a fresh start after seven years (and several injury setbacks) in Washington.*
>
> *At Philadelphia Union training camp, he told the gathered media: 'Seven years in one place, it was a long time. I got into too much of a routine, and I wasn't pushing myself every day like I know I could. And I knew Philly's a place where I can change things up and give me a fresh start. ... The biggest thing for me – every time I walked into that stadium, I thought about injuries. ... It got very monotonous for me in DC, and I felt like I needed a shakeup.'*
>
> Steve Goff, "Washington Post Soccer Insider"

Athletes, coaches, general managers, and everyone involved in a soccer team knows they will likely be fired at some point. Those who don't get fired, retire. No one involved in a sports team expects to spend their entire working careers with that one organization. A team is made up of the best performers available and affordable at the moment.

Even in this expectation of departures, firings, and demotions there is loyalty and comradery on soccer teams. Thierry Henry, an Arsenal legend, started his career at a French team called Monaco, then went to the Italian team Juventus, then Arsenal, then Barcelona in Spain, and then the New York Red Bulls in the US before he retired. After leaving Arsenal for Spain and America, Henry returned to London to work with Arsenal's youth teams and with an eye to coaching the first team one day.[1] Henry is no less beloved because he neither began nor finished his career in North London; indeed he is more valuable because he learned from other systems, coaches, and teams. DC United's squad has featured stars like Jamie Moreno and Bobby Boswell who played in Washington, DC, left for other teams, and then came back to the nation's capital. There were no hard feelings when the players left and there were no awkward moments when they returned – it's the nature of the game.

Soccer takes the temporary-ness of assignments a step further than other sports. It is common practice for soccer teams to loan players to other teams in other countries, in lower divisions of the same league, or even to other teams in the same division of the same league. In 2015 a young American player named DeAndre Yedlin was sold from the Seattle Sounders of Major League Soccer to Tottenham Hotspur Football Club of the British Premier League. They promptly loaned him to Sunderland Association Football Club, a rival team in the same league.[2] Spurs (as Tottenham is called) already had players in Yedlin's position who were better than he was, so he probably wouldn't play for them immediately. In loaning him to a team that needed his skills rather than making him sit on the bench all season, Spurs were able to get a little money from Sunderland in exchange for his services and Yedlin got valuable playing time and experience.

*... there is a comradery/social dynamic that is important – where players/individuals care about each other – know some of the personal stuff in each other's lives and take that into consideration.*
Alan Dietrich, Chief Operating Officer, Sporting KC

While recreational league teams do not engage in such complex maneuvers there is still the expectation that one may change teams, and there are usually no hard feelings because of that movement. I was on three teams in my first five years of playing in a local over-45 league. The first team folded, the second team was quite good but not a group of guys I wanted to play with every Sunday. On my first team I typically played at center back because that's what they needed and I started every game. When I was playing poorly I was pulled out of the game, and when needed I played in different positions. On my second team I switched to outside back and played just about every minute of every game because I was one of two people on the team with the skills needed in that position (the other person with those skills played at the other outside back position). On my current team not only do I not play the whole game, I often don't start. If the team were a family my getting benched so Kevin could start would be cause for drunken fights at holidays and possibly daytime television appearances. I like my teammates, but very rarely see any of them off the field. We laugh and joke more often than not as we warm up and after the games, but that's it. When a guy gets hurt or his family has something bad happen, we support him. When the captain's daughter was accepted to her first-choice college where she would be playing soccer, we applauded. But I played with Arturo Sarukhan for years before I learned he was a leading Mexican diplomat – and even that I only learned because I saw him in a charity match not because of what we shared on the field. All nice and friendly, but far from familial.

For some managers a company is a family that cares about each other and happens to make money as it does so – the company actually makes more money because it is a family. The reasoning is that families work together because they want to, not because they have to. Family members care about each other, support each other simply because they are family. This is of course nonsense. If we have learned anything from prime time police dramas it's that a lot of people are nice to their parents, grandparents, and assorted aunts and uncles because some of them might be rich or have a great piece of jewelry or vacation house that we desperately want when they die. It is also inaccurate for the other reasons outlined in this chapter – after all this is a book about organizations and teams, not complicated plots to make it look like Uncle Lou died in a tragic boating accident rather than from arsenic in his vintage cognac.

Setting aside the disturbing notion that one's family should be the means to the end of generating wealth for someone else, wanting to call a staff a family is understandable. The best jobs are not those you show up to, do the minimum not to get fired, and leave the moment the clock strikes five. You spend a third of your day, half of your waking hours (at least) going to work, at work, and going home – one would hope there is more to it than soul-crushing ambivalence or antipathy in exchange for what is likely too small a paycheck to cover your expenses and put away a little for retirement or a rainy day. A lot of people are forced by circumstance or as the result of poor choices to have those jobs, but if you are reading this book odds are good you do not view your job this way, or at least that you don't want to.

But companies are not families. Parents cannot fire children who do not do their chores and (hopefully) your family doesn't hand out most valuable sibling awards with preferred seating at the dinner table and a sign on the chair that says "reserved for the family member of the month." When a family's finances get tight the youngest child isn't let go. The point of a family is not to maximize returns for investors; the point of a family is the family. To call your staff a family is to set you both up for failure and disappointment. Your job cannot fulfill your emotional needs and you are not responsible for fulfilling the emotional needs of your boss or your staff. If a company were a family then when someone left for another job it would be the equivalent of your daughter abandoning you because she liked the other parents better (maybe they do not require her to do the dishes or they have Netflix), and firing an underperformer or laying off someone who is good but no longer needed is equivalent to leaving your sweet old uncle at a rest stop and driving away while he's in the men's room.

Families support each other from the outside world – the point of a company is the outside world. Families focus in, successful organizations focus out.

Another way to conceive of a company or unit is as a team. Members of the team and the coaches support each other, are often friends, and work to make each other better. They may go to each other's parties, their kids play together, and they may come to each other's aid when a family tragedy strikes. A team can be seen as something of a middle ground between a family and just a place you go to put bolts on manifolds. Like a family, a team is supportive, works together, and is loyal. Unlike a family, a team is goal driven, does not assume unconditional support, and can change. An additional advantage of the team metaphor is that on a team everyone has a role and everyone's role contributes to the team's goals. Families care about each other even though not everyone helps out as much as they should, but unlike individual mercenaries teams have a shared identity that is greater than any one person. You are invested first in the goal, and then in each other as a means of achieving that goal.

Conceived of in this way, a company or unit is a group of professionals who come together to achieve a task. Your colleagues are more than people who happen to sit next to you, but less than your aunt. Your obligation is to work together to achieve a common purpose, which requires you to be respectful but does not require you to be friends.

Thinking of a company as a team and not a family allows you to be more honest about who should be promoted, retained, or released. We have all worked in places with colleagues who are nice but not up to the task and who no one seems to be able to fire. If an organization is viewed as a family the mediocre but enthusiastic and friendly staff member who keeps a jar of candy on his desk is tolerated. No one wants to get rid of him because he is such a nice guy and is not doing anything clearly wrong to merit dismissal, any more than you do not invite your sweet but a little lost little brother to Thanksgiving even if all he ever brings are chips and his boyfriend who only eats gluten-free, free range, virgin tofu. If an organization is a team and not a family, those underperformers – even those with great attitudes and endless chocolate – are more likely to be asked to leave. Similarly, the outstanding performer who may not be the best liked is more likely to get promoted. On teams the metric is performance within the team toward the goal.

> *Acknowledging that your employee might leave is how you build*
> *the relationship that convinces great people to stay.*
> Reid Hoffman, The Alliance visual summary[3]

Few of your employees will spend their entire career at your company. You want to hire people who will be around long enough to make an impact, and you certainly want to be sure that the time and effort you put into integrating a new employee is worth it, but you probably do not want to hire a lot of people whose career ambition is to get, and stay in, the job for which you are hiring (especially if it's an entry-level or mid-career position). As a team you will be more likely to be successful if everyone understands that everyone is probably only at the organization for a limited amount of time. After some number of years it is likely, and probably healthy, for an employee to move on to a new organization. If that person does so with your support – as a team member moving to a rival team or different league, rather than as a son leaving to pick new parents – that employee is much more likely to want to come back in a more

senior position, bringing your firm valuable experience and expertise. Further, if you treat your employees' career ambitions honestly from the outset, and help them achieve those goals, word will get around and you are likely to attract top talent that is as ambitious as it is expert.

## Locker Room Notes for Managers

Treat your managers and staff as a team, not as a family or group of individuals who happen to park in the same garage.

Do not expect either your boss or your reports to like you. It is nicer to be liked than not, but you should turn to your friends for affection and not to those whom you manage or by whom you are managed. Keep professional boundaries and be aware of the difference between friends and subordinates. Be sure you evaluate your reports based on their performance, not on your affection for them (or lack thereof).

Do not mistake your team for your family. Don't call them your family and don't treat them like family. Do not ask them to socialize with you for fun, be aware of personal boundaries, and don't expect your staff to like you (and don't worry if you don't especially like them).

As you evaluate, promote, and fire people be sure to do so because of their success or failure to work with the team to advance your shared goal. Do not fire or fail to promote someone because you don't like them or they never come to happy hour, and do not hang on to under-performers because they are nice or you feel a personal bond.

## Locker Room Notes for Staff

Do not try to be your boss's friend. Be someone on whom your colleagues and managers can rely, be supportive and collegial, but be aware of boundaries. If you get promoted it should be because you're doing a good job at something which needs to be done, not because you're popular – and if you get let go it should be because you are failing at your assigned task or the task you are doing is no longer needed, not because your boss doesn't like you. Getting promoted does not mean supervisors will be more loyal to you, and getting fired or laid off is not an indictment of you as a person. Your company doesn't care about you as a person; it cares about you as a contributor, so focus on being a good contributor.

## Endnotes

1.  Most soccer teams around the world have a number of teams for different age groups, starting as young as under-eight and many run academies that are akin to boarding schools for potential soccer stars. In Germany many of the teams in the top division also field teams in the lower divisions and in the US. Major League Soccer teams have academies as well as affiliations with professional and semi-professional teams in lower American divisions, much like baseball teams have minor league franchises. Both players and coaches work their way up through the ranks.

2.  Soccer players who are under contract to play for one team are regularly bought and sold rather than traded as is the norm in most US sports. There are internationally agreed upon windows in the summer and winter during which teams may offer transfer payments – many running into many tens of millions of dollars – to other teams to acquire players. The bulk of the transfer fee goes to the team selling the player's contract, while a portion of the fee goes to the player. Teams are under no obligation to sell players, but sometimes the money can be too hard to refuse. The highest transfer fee ever paid, as of January 2016, was paid by the Spanish side Real Madrid to Tottenham Hotspur for Gareth Bale, something in the neighborhood of $122.5 million in 2013 – that wasn't his salary, that's what Real paid Spurs for the rights to pay Bale's salary to play in Spain.

3. LinkedIn cofounder Reid Hoffman talks about this as a "tour of duty" approach to employee management and development – another useful metaphor for organizations.

## Chapter 8

# Manage Your Strengths and Weaknesses

Every player does some things well and some things poorly. The best players find ways to use their strengths and adjust for their weaknesses. The best managers and staff similarly know what they do well, and do that. They also know what they do poorly and work with their colleagues to compensate for those weaknesses.

> He's played to our strengths. He's just built on being a hard-working team and not giving the opposition anything, counter attacking and causing problems.
> Michael Morrison, captain of Birmingham City in England's second division praising his manager, "Birmingham City: Harry Redknapp has galavanised Blues says skipper Morrison"

> To be a self-aware leader you must know who you are, before you can look at yourself in the context of your company or in the context of your peers. I don't believe you can be an effective leader without emotional intelligence and self-awareness. Understanding yourself and your own limitations – what you're good at, what you're not good at, is critical to ensure you are surrounding yourself with the right people that may be leverage for your weaknesses or enhance your strengths," says Dan Brodie, CIO of BuildDirect.
> Rich Hein, In "16 Traits of Great It Leaders"

"Play within yourself" is a phrase you hear a lot in sports. Playing within yourself means knowing what you are good at and doing that. It also means knowing what you are not good at, getting better at those things, and finding others who can compensate for your weaknesses.

I am relatively quick, relatively fit, a decent passer, and am taller than many soccer players (note the liberal use of the term "relatively" – I find that I am faster and fitter when I play on my over-45 team than I am when I play pickup with recent college grads). I am not the guy doing the highlight-reel moves that leave defenders dizzy, and I am not a great shooter. I slip by the occasional unsuspecting defender and score the occasional goal, but by and large I focus on the parts of the game I do relatively well at and find ways to deal with the things I do poorly.

> *If I'm slower than the guy I'm covering, I play position rather than man to man, which requires self-honesty, knowing your weakness.*
> Roger Frank, former semi-professional player, investment fund manager and serial entrepreneur

I also work on my weaknesses on the field. I exercise to keep my fitness sharp for games, and which helps compensate for my aging. When I kick a ball around before a game or against a wall I try to use my weaker left foot, practice turning, and otherwise work on those skills on which I need work. I even briefly had a soccer trainer. Knowing where I need to improve puts me in a position to get better. Ignoring my shortcomings – or worse, believing I do not have any – guarantees I will never progress as a player and therefore never be as valuable a teammate as I could be.

When people show up on a soccer field they tend to put themselves in a position to succeed. If asked where they like to play they will say a position at which they are good and not one at which they are bad. It is pretty clear pretty fast if someone is lying – as the saying goes, you can't hide slow.

Taking that approach to a job interview, pitch meeting, or performance review can feel risky. Our first instinct is to say "of course I/we can do that!" and worry about making the claim true later on. A lot of interviewers have stopped asking potential employees "what is your greatest weakness" because the answer is inevitably something like, "I work too hard," or "I bake too much at home and end up having to give away cookies at the office." But of course not all of us are good at every part of every job. I have professional strengths and weaknesses just as I do on the soccer field. Those weaknesses can become pretty apparent pretty quickly, and if I am not honest about them my project will suffer, the organization's goals will not be met, and I will likely get fired. If I am honest about those weaknesses I can compensate with my strengths, work on getting better, and rely on my colleagues to support me. Your shortcomings are as obvious in the office as they are on the field – you can either own them or you can be punished by them. I know those I hire will be better at some things than they are at others, they will have strengths and weaknesses. When I hire people, I look for those whose strengths compensate for my weaknesses and other gaps on the team, and whose weaknesses will be compensated for by others.

Note that "compensate" is not the same as "ignore." If I ignore the fact that I am slower than people half my age on the soccer field my team gives up goals. But if I compensate, I cover space rather than the opponent, or work with my teammates to adjust the system.

*One of the hardest things to do in life is to be completely honest with yourself about yourself. It requires total truthfulness about strengths and weakness regardless of how those revelations make us feel about ourselves. Nevertheless, as entrepreneurs, it's probably our greatest weapon in putting together a great team of people to build our vision into a viable company.*
Douglas Paul "Manager Know Thyself: Identifying your Strengths and Weaknesses for Better or Worse"

In an office it means the same thing. If you are expected to give regular presentations and you are not a good public speaker, you can either continue to blow presentations by continuing to do what you are bad at, come down with a sudden death in the family or a highly contagious deadly disease every time you have to speak, or find ways to work with your colleagues to work around your weakness. The first two approaches ignore a soccer or system approach to work, and inevitably result in failure. The last option – work with your colleagues – is the heart of the soccer approach and can lead to success.

For example, I am a good public speaker and am pretty quick on my feet (somewhat ironically given it's a weakness on the field). But I am terrible at making PowerPoint presentations and other slide decks. For a while I tried to ignore the weakness by bragging about it. As a result, every time I gave a presentation I was highlighting a weakness. Audiences expect slides; not having slides (or having terrible slides) meant that I was letting my audience down before I even opened my mouth. Now if I have to give a presentation, I ask others to write the presentation around my notes or around our conversations, or I take a first pass at it and turn the presentation over to those more skilled than I am. By focusing on the goal (a successful presentation) rather than on myself, I do a better job of advancing the team's objectives. I once had to give a short presentation about my division's goals, how those goals advanced the organizational mission, and the resources needed to achieve those goals. I sat down with my team, we talked about the presentation, and I did a very rough draft slide deck based on my notes. Some on my team were skilled at making slide presentations and they took over. The result was a stronger presentation and a stronger team because we all worked together on our shared goal; the process of creating the presentation made the presentation better and the unit stronger. It also had the personal benefit of helping me get better at constructing slide presentations because I could see the thought process and elements that went into creating good visual support for my presentation. By owning my shortcoming I ensured a better outcome for the unit and empowered my staff, which made them better, and got better myself.

## Locker Room Notes for Managers

Be honest about your strengths and weaknesses with yourself and your staff.

Put people in positions that play to their strengths, and find others whose strengths compensate for team members' weaknesses.

## Locker Room Notes for Staff

Be honest about your strengths and weaknesses with yourself and your boss.

Put yourself in positions that play to your strengths and find ways to both adjust for and work on your weaknesses.

# Chapter 9

# Respect, Competition, Cooperation

Soccer relies on both competition against and cooperation with the opposing team. Rec league games require helping local league officials, and pickup soccer relies on ad hoc cooperation. Being a good colleague at work is professionally useful, and is the right thing to do.

> *The exchanging of jerseys at the end of a soccer match is a longtime ritual that is well established in the sport, even as it has evolved ...*

> *"It's just a sign of respect," said Clint Mathis, who scored for the United States in the 2002 World Cup. "You're out there trying to kick each other and kill each other, but when the game's said and done, it's back to being friends."*
> Billy Witz, The New York Times

> *Helping up-and-comers or even longstanding competition can occasionally be a hard thing to do, but in the right instances there are good reasons to do it anyway.*
> Robert Tuchman "Five Reasons You Need to Work With Your Competitors"

Soccer relies on competition against other teams and cooperation with your own teammates. It also relies on competition with your teammates and cooperation with competitors. To succeed, this competition and cooperation needs to respect both other players and the game itself. Successful organizations share this approach.

The quality of a teammate is often seen in the locker room or on the sidelines. Coaches want players who are positive forces in the locker room. These are players who take responsibility for their mistakes, encourage their teammates, and keep everyone focused. Similarly, coaches want to avoid players who blame others for their mistakes and whose attitude brings everyone down. Just as an enthusiastic teammate can help lift a team, a negative attitude can poison a team.

There is an additional twist to cooperation and competition in soccer that is not seen as much in other sports. Partner at the Mayer Brown law firm and former US Men's National Team player Amr Aly points out that professional teams are increasingly made up of players from all over the world. Players who may be teammates on their national team during World Cup qualifying or a regional tournament one weekend, may be opponents in their professional league the next weekend. Top players learn when and how to compete, and when and how to cooperate.

A bad game in the pros can get someone sent to the bench or cut, so there is a pretty strong motivation to keep focused and positive even if your teammates are not. And ultimately no one would be a professional if they relied exclusively on others to keep them going. In rec league soccer all that is at stake is a bit of ego and bragging rights; if you are tired or having a bad game it is easy to let your quality slip or just take yourself out. And for us weekend warriors a few words one way or the other can make a big difference – it is much more fun to spend a few hours on a Sunday with people who are positive and supportive than it is with players who are negative and insulting. Positive players help their teammates play better. A simple "bad luck, keep attacking" can go a long way when you're tired – and shouts of "stop screwing up and play faster" can be demoralizing and lead to even worse play. A joke after a botched play or scuffed shot can diffuse tension and help everyone relax, and relaxed players are better players.

Of course locker rooms are not always joyous places full of orange slices and trophies for effort. Even on the field players scream at each other for slights real and imagined. For professionals the stakes can be incredibly high and pressure incredibly intense. Relegation from a top division to a lower one can cost a team tens of millions of dollars, and promotion can mean adding tens of millions of dollars to the bottom line. Qualifying for European-wide competitions such as the Champions League can mean many tens of millions of dollars more. This is on top of the contract incentives, endorsements, and the competitive nature of anyone who reaches the top levels of a sport. High stakes bring strong emotions, which can turn into nasty exchanges.

Sometimes these exchanges turn into fights that get into the press. They can disrupt team morale, undermine the unit, and make the team less successful. But the dust-ups can also have a positive effect on performance. Professional athletes know they are expected to excel and that sometimes getting shouted at can be a good motivator. None of us wants to let teammates whom we respect down. We may hate to admit it, but sometimes getting berated by a teammate (or colleague) can be what we need to keep focused and do our best.

The players need to feel and demonstrate trust and respect for the shouting to be productive and not destructive. As a player, I am OK with getting chewed out by a teammate who is working as hard as I am and who I know values my contribution to the team. On the other hand, I am not OK with getting yelled at by someone I do not respect, who I do not think is carrying his weight, or who does not want me around at all. Good teammates are always respectful but need not always be nice.

*A good football team like a good management team will use conflict to drive to a better result, but the fundamental requirement is that respect exists in order to have positive conflict.*
Michael Williamson, Chief Strategy Officer F.C. Internazionale Milano (Inter Milan)

There is a fine line between being a strong competitor and being a jerk. There are people who start with disrespect and go downhill from there. Their first response to every idea is negative, they are the first to say "I told you so," and they never take responsibility for mistakes or failures. These are the people who complain in meetings and who snap at their colleagues. If they see a half empty glass, they go out of their way to drain what's left. These colleagues can sometimes be stars in their fields, have tremendous knowledge, or be astonishing deal-closers. But they're jerks, and jerks make everyone around them worse.

Successful soccer players and teams compete and cooperate not just with each other, but with other teams against whom they are competing as well. Even in the pros, where the stakes are high and the pressure intense, players often kick the ball out of bounds when someone on the opposing team is obviously injured, and when the game resumes the team putting the ball back into play plays it to the team that kicked it out. This isn't a rule, it's just what's done.

In the middle of a heated game between the Philadelphia Union and DC United in the middle of the 2017 Major League Soccer Season, the Union's Haris Medunjanin was fouled by DC United's Luciano Acosta. The referee deemed the foul worthy of a red card, which would have sent Acosta to the showers and meant that DC would have played with 10 men for the game's remaining 16 or so minutes. It also would have meant that DC's most creative player would miss the next game. The stakes were pretty high. Both teams were near the bottom of the standings and both needed a win or at least a tie. Nevertheless, Medunjanin told the ref that while Acosta pushed him over, the foul was not harsh enough to warrant a red card. The ref conferred with the players, and agreed with Medunjanin. The ref changed his initial call, Acosta remained on the field and the game continued with both sides at full strength (Philadelphia went on to win 1-0).

This is not how it always goes of course. Lots of pros play dirty and some of the faked injuries and fouls in soccer rival those of trained stage fighters (and the over-acting can rival that of your nine-year-old's dramatic death scene in a school play). But by and large the players play within both the laws and norms of the game.

Most rec league soccer games are played on fields without permanent goals, nets, corner flags, or lines. Every Saturday or Sunday morning someone who works for the league or local parks and recreation department gets to the field before that day's games start and sets up the field, and when the games are done takes everything down. They clear litter and rocks and make the rectangle that is a soccer field a safe place to play. The people doing this work tend to be retirees, college kids, or others for whom a couple of extra bucks makes a difference. If your team is scheduled for the first game and you arrive early, you are expected to help set up the field. If your team plays the last game of the day you are expected to help take the field down. You should help because the help would be appreciated and because you can. When you see litter on a field, you pick it up and throw it away – you have to jog around a bit to warm up, you may as well jog toward to the litter and then the trash can.

Pickup soccer is played wherever there is space and people. Sometimes games are on school or community fields with goals, but more often than not games are played on what everyone playing agrees is a fair patch of mostly flat ground. Some regular games bring their own miniature folding goals that people in the group pitch in to pay for, but goals are usually garbage cans or people's gym bags. A bunch of years ago I bought miniature orange cones and keep them in my soccer bag to mark corners or goals as needed. For a while I was part of a regular Saturday morning game for which I bought folding goals that I brought every weekend and stored in my garage. I asked the game's regulars to chip in $20 each to defray the cost, and most did.[1] No one asks you to help set up or put away the goals, or if your bag can be a goal – you throw your bag down, bring out the cones or set up the goal.

This is not how all rec league or pickup play goes. A Brazilian once told me he hated soccer because his best friend growing up got stabbed over a local pickup game that someone put money on,[2] and I left an over-45 rec league team after a successful season because they insisted on arguing with the other team, the referees, and each other. Those games are not a lot of fun and mostly what you learn from them is to never play in those games or on those teams. They are the companies that top talent keeps leaving, and that eventually can only hire those willing to put up with the place until they can get a better job.

The other half of competitive cooperation is external, against (and with) other teams. Competition only works if opposing players agree to follow the same rules and behave within the same norms. I can get pretty competitive on the field – one reason I like playing defense is that's a relatively physical position – but I also try to be a good cooperator. I chat with the woman who checks in the over-45 teams in Montgomery County and thank her for looking after us, and I make sure the guy I just knocked off the ball is OK before continuing play. Before and after, and even during, games I talk to players on the other team. Playing hard does not have to be the same as being unpleasant.

*How To Become The Most Well-Liked Person In The Office: Building better relationships with your coworkers can do more for your career than just making your workday more pleasant.*

*"Nothing derails your likability more than ego," says Jennifer Blank, HR manager at McGarrah Jessee. Roll up your sleeves whenever needed. Offer to help others complete time-sensitive projects, even when it's not your job. "You'll earn gold stars when the folks you work with know you've got everyone's best interest at*

*heart, and that you can be counted on to contribute your fair share to the workload," says Blank.*
Fast Company

This is as easy to do in the office as it is on the field. Being a good colleague can have professional benefits and advance the organization's goals. By constantly thinking "how can I help improve the space in which I'm working? How can I help my colleagues do their jobs?" you are constantly thinking about the success of the organization and your role in the system; you are finding ways to support the system that is advancing the shared goal. Rather than just thinking about your piece of the goal, you are thinking about your role in the larger connected system. In addition you are demonstrating that you are a good, thoughtful, colleague. People like to work with good, thoughtful colleagues and will want to work with you – which increases your chances for success as an individual. By putting the system first you benefit the system as well as yourself.

Coalition meetings, ad hoc working groups, internal "tiger teams," and the like are the business equivalent of rec league soccer and pickup games – they may or may not happen regularly, and are basically casual. Some groups and meetings come and go as needed with no set schedule or leader. Sometimes the meetings have a formal chair but participants can move in and out. They are ad hoc or "semi hoc," falling short of Board of Directors presentations or quarterly earnings calls. The same rules apply to these meetings as apply to rec league and pickup soccer.

If you bring a cup into a conference room, take it with you when you leave or throw it away. If you enter a conference room in which people have left coffee cups, take them with you or throw them away when you leave. If you attend a meeting and someone brings you coffee, ask where the kitchen is on the way out so you can wash the cup. Make coffee if you are the first one in, and if you finish the coffee make a new pot. While you are waiting for the coffee to brew, empty the office dishwasher. Use coasters – there's no disadvantage, you help preserve the look of the table, and using a coaster demonstrates that you are both thoughtful and civilized. If you see litter in the hall, pick it up and throw it away. If you spill something, wipe it up. You shouldn't have to be asked to help keep the shared space of an office neat, and you certainly shouldn't have to be asked to pick up after yourself. These are things you should do because it is part of what makes a shared space work.

It is easy to think "team" in sports; they are called sports teams, after all. Sports teams are in a relatively small space shouting at each other for relatively short periods of time, so there is not a lot of time or space to drift off in your own private musings. It can be tougher at an organization which may have office doors that close others out and you in. You are also at work a lot and you can't be social all of the time; you have your specific projects and deadlines you have to meet, many of your colleagues may be on different floors, in different buildings, time zones, or countries. It can be difficult to remain team focused under these conditions. Which is why it is all the more important to behave "exceedingly teamly" (to steal a phrase from a former colleague). Because the system focus can be difficult to maintain you should make an extra effort to maintain it. Doing the little things like picking up after other people's meetings or volunteering to help a group project, can help everyone stay engaged with each other and develop the habit of working as part of an interconnected system.

Being a good colleague at work sometimes means disagreeing – even strongly. As leading behavioral experts Cass Sunstein and Reid Hastie note, "A confident, cohesive, but error-prone group is nothing to celebrate." Agreement can actually make things worse by giving the group and leadership a false sense of security and surety in the decision.

*The best teams to hold each other accountable. Feedback and*
*criticism is part of the day, it is the only way that we grow.*
Ben Olsen, Head coach of DC United and former Olympic
and World Cup player

In the last year of President Obama's administration the
Commissioner of the US Food and Drug Administration
created a senior advisor role for me, a position that required the
President appointing me to the federal Senior Executive Service.
My job was to help the Commissioner advance White House and
FDA priorities before Obama's term ended. One of the many
things I loved about working with the Commissioner is that
he encouraged respectful disagreement and honest discussion.
He invited criticism of his ideas, and encouraged everyone
in meetings to weigh in on topics – especially if they had a
different perspective. (His approach could be because he was a
cardiologist and benign niceties that lead to bad decisions can
kill patients.) One result was that everyone who participated in
the meetings was prepared – there are a lot of really smart people
at the FDA, including the Commissioner; if you were going to
engage in an argument you had better know your stuff. I was
in a lot of meetings during which I disagreed with some of my
colleagues, and those discussions could get heated. But everyone
in those meetings also respected each other and the arguments
were about policy and action and not about the people making
the arguments. It was not always fun; I still disagree with some
of the outcomes of those conversations, and not every decision
may have been the right one, but every decision in which I was
involved was made by people honestly pushing each other to
find the best decision possible. The cooperative outcome – FDA
policy – was made by people respectfully pushing each other's
ideas around.

Sometimes business competitors need to cooperate with each
other. There are legal limits to this cooperation (there is a fine

line between cooperating and colluding), and of course good commercial reasons not to cooperate. But competition is not the same as enmity. One can compete and still treat others with respect.

*I was a fierce competitor on the field, but once you're off the field you put that stuff down. As a litigator when I take a deposition I go head to head with an opposing attorney, competing fiercely. Then we share a cab on the way to the airport.*

Amr Aly, partner at the Mayer Brown law firm and former member of US Men's National Team and former professional player

I managed the re-election campaign for one of the most vulnerable members of Congress. The campaign drew national attention and a lot of money, and was pretty intense. But every week the opponent's campaign manager and I made time to talk on the phone, and if something especially egregious happened, we didn't hesitate to call each other. A few days after the election (which my candidate won going away) we met for lunch to talk about the campaign and share stories. We went at the campaign hammer and tongs, but neither of us lost sight of the other as people cooperating in a competitive system.

One famous example of this cooperation was after the Twin Towers were taken down in the 9/11 terrorist attack. Financial firms gave office space to rivals whose offices were destroyed in the attack. Rather than simply gain from a tragedy that had befallen their competitors, these companies chose to cooperate for the good of the financial industry more broadly and because it was the right thing to do.

Such an approach is routine in sports. Most leagues have competition committees, whose members are representatives of the teams in those leagues. The committee comes together to set the rules by which everyone will play and through which the league can succeed. The teams compete on the field or court, but cooperate to make that competition successful.

## Locker Room Notes for Managers

Be seen to be acting for the good of the team – pick up after yourself, use a coaster, model good behavior. Your staff (and their staffs) will do as you do.

Reward those who go out of the way to support the group by calling them out in meetings and making it part of their regular reviews.

Invite and encourage respectful disagreement and competition. Shut it down as soon the disagreement and competition become personal and lacks respect.

## Locker Room Notes for Staff

Be seen to be acting for the good of the team – pick up after yourself, use a coaster, model good behavior.

Respectfully challenge decisions by others on your team. Make it clear you are ensuring every angle is considered fully before a decision is made or action taken, that you are not wedded to your challenge, and that you respect the others on the team. And then push.

## Endnotes

1. Everyone who rides in my wife's car, which was mine when I bought the goals, asks what all the white marks on the ceiling and walls of the car are. The answer is scratches from the PVC piping that made up the superstructure of the goals. They were great goals, and folded up pretty small, but there was still some collateral automotive damage.

2. A Brazilian saying he hates soccer is a bit like an Englishman saying he hates tea or an American says he doesn't like apple pie – it seems somehow treasonous to admit such a thing even if it's true.

## Chapter 10

# Goals

In addition to the goal of scoring goals, soccer players set interim and personal goals that make it more likely that goals will be scored. The best managers and staff set personal and system goals that, when combined, make it more likely that the organization will achieve its ultimate goal.

*In 126 Years, English Football Has Seen 13,475 Nil-Nil Draws.*
Oliver Roeder, FiveThirtyEight.com

*In explaining one of the parallels between restaurant management and soccer, DC restaurateur and former professional player Ari Gejdenson borrows an example from Fred Kofman's book Conscious Business and applies it to restaurants. Kofman writes that in soccer, the whole team has to have a single incentive to win – if forwards are rewarded for scoring goals, while defenders are rewarded for preventing them, forwards will fight for a 5-4 loss while defenders would rather a 1-0 win. In applying this to his business, Ari says that in a restaurant the goal needs to be the customer experience; if a chef is rewarded only for food excellence he may make a diner wait until a dish is perfect and if a server is rewarded only for the number of customers he serves he will rush people through a meal. On the field and in a restaurant, success requires that everyone on the team has to be working toward the same, single, goal.*

Goals are the point of soccer. But those goals are notoriously difficult to come by – according to a database of 188,060 professional games in England between 1888 and 2014 the most common final score was 1-0. In more than 13,000 of those games the final score was 0-0.

In soccer it can be difficult to measure specific statistics on the way to neither team appearing to accomplish anything. This book is based on the premise that soccer is a system that relies on interaction of all of its parts through both time and space, making measurement even tougher. Worse yet, soccer players do things that may never be seen and may be difficult to measure. Companies like OPTA do a good job of tracking relevant data, which can help managers make informed decisions, but the nature of the sport makes little goals that add up to the ultimate goal of scoring goals tricky – especially since so few goals are ever scored.

There are some obvious things one can measure in a soccer game – shots on target, assists, tackles won[1], completed pass percentage, and so forth. Each of these are small goals that help add up to the larger goal of a victory. But those statistics can be deceptive – the completed pass percentage might be high because the player only made easy passes or never tried to dribble with the ball, and shots on target could have been at the expense of passing the ball to players in a better position to score. Rather than measure the elements that lead to victory – the goal of the goals – such measurements can become ends in themselves. Poorly established goals can lead to players getting rewarded for doing that which is easy to measure rather than that which helps the team succeed.

Statistics about where the play is (passing, dribbling, shooting, tackling) can also be incomplete because they do not measure the impact a player has where the play isn't. For example it can be difficult to measure when a player runs to create space for other players to move in to, where they shift to cover a gap, or on the field instructions and guidance they provide their teammates. Poorly designed metrics can fail to measure the important things, which can result in coaches not rewarding those things and therefore players no longer doing them. Worse, poorly designed metrics can measure the wrong things, leading coaches and players to actively be counter-productive. Different incentives for different players – goals scored versus goals presented, for example – can undermine success entirely.

But good measurement of good minor goals is important so coaches can assemble the best teams and get the most out of their players. Players need incremental goals so they can track their own progress. Weekend soccer duffers like me need measurement other than the number of goals our team scores to have a roadmap to improvement.

*... there is an importance of measurable [goals] in soccer and business beyond win/loss and goals scored – for example, distance travelled, speeds, distance kicked/thrown, possession, assists, etc. – picking the right measurable per position/individual is vital.*

Alan Dietrich, Chief Operating Officer, Sporting KC

The easily measurable goals can be in the context of the larger goal – the number of passes completed that led to an attack, or shots on goal that required a goalkeeper to move to save, and so forth. Goals can also be different for different players and in different positions, and goals can be different during practice than during a game. A defender can set a personal goal of limiting the number of times someone runs past him with the ball, or how many passes he intercepts. I'm a reasonable passer, but am not very good with the ball at my feet so I sometimes set personal goals of taking players on during pickup games (not enough times that I cost my team, but enough so I can practice for when it matters more in league games). A midfielder who doesn't take many shots can set a goal of four shots a game, and a forward can commit to making three defensive plays in his own half. Players can also commit to making runs that create options for their teammates, setting a target for the numbers of times they will pull someone on the other team out of position. All of these smaller and specific goals only make sense if they are in the service of the ultimate team goal of winning games.

Even in the complex and fluid system which is soccer, there are specific benchmarks one can set to measure performance and get better.

Organizations and industries can be like soccer in this regard. Companies are complex systems that move through time and space; they have lots of people doing lots of things that may be easily measured but may not advance the organization's goal, and they may have lots of people doing critical things that are difficult to measure. Some statistics are easy to track – deals closed (both in absolute terms and as a percentage of pitches), products produced, revenue to expenses, year-to-year growth, and so forth. As in soccer, some of these measurements can be deceptive. For example, sales can put short-term gains over long-term investment or put getting clients in the door over keeping the clients once they've signed on.

Those who do not directly do those things that are most easily measured may not have a clear connection between their day-to-day jobs and the organization's goals, which can make it more difficult for both managers and staff. Staff may not know exactly what they should be doing day-to-day, and managers may end up measuring the wrong things because they can't figure out what the right things to measure are.

Everyone who takes a course on research methods hears a variation of the same story to explain the importance of your measurement tool measuring what you're looking for and not just what is easy to find – A policeman approaches a drunk who is searching for something under a streetlamp. "Can I help you find something?" the cop asks. "I dropped my wallet over there," replies the drunk, pointing to a dark part of the street. "So why aren't you looking where you dropped it?" the policeman asks. "The light's better," replies the drunk.

*If you want to build a solid and strong project, you must think on the long term, and you should be ambitious. Thinking only in the short team is the most common mistake.*

Alex Aranzábal Mínguez, Partner AYA – Aguirre y Aranzabal and former President of SD Eibar in La Liga

The trick is not setting goals; the trick is setting the right goals and measuring against them. For example, it can be easy to measure an increase in social media reach by counting the numbers of followers and times something is shared – but that reach may or may not mean one is reaching decision makers or customers in ways that will make them purchase the product or buy the service. More difficult to measure is what you really need to know: who is following and sharing, and what they are doing with the information. But in setting the first as a benchmark for your media team you are distracting them from doing what you really want done: advancing the organizational goal. It's like counting shots versus shots on target or shots to goals-scored ratios; if you count all the shots, your players will be aiming at the other team's goal from wherever they happen to be standing on the field, and those shots will come at the expense of advancing the team's actual goal, which is goals. If you have a player who shoots on average twice a game and who, on average, scores a goal a game, you are in a much more likely position to win than you are if you have a player who shoots a dozen times a game but only scores once every other game.

A friend who runs a national organization was frustrated with some of his staff around the country because they were "checking boxes" rather than advancing the organization's goals. The big goals of the organization were difficult to measure and took time, so the organization set interim benchmarks to measure progress. The problem is that the staff had begun to focus on the interim steps rather than the goal itself. Real progress was difficult to see, so they looked where it was easy even if where they were looking didn't necessarily matter that much. Like a soccer player who points to the number of passes he completes as evidence that he's helping the team win, these staff were mistaking what they could measure with what mattered.

For example, if you measure social media, measure who follows you, rather than how many follow you. Set a goal of one re-tweet or social media mention a month (or week or day) by a leading industry commentator or thought leader. If you measure press clips, focus on those in publications read by your customers or those who you need to succeed; count sections of newspapers you want to be in to be sure you are reaching your audience where and when they are thinking about your field.

There are all sorts of small goals that managers can set for their staff who may not have an outward facing role that can have big consequences. For example, if a manager has a staff member who is continually at the office 11 hours a day, or who emails late at night and weekends, that should raise a red flag. Everyone needs downtime to recover and be at their best, and continued 55-plus hour weeks are counterproductive. Odds are good the person is not being as efficient as she should be at the office, could be burning out, and is almost certainly setting a bad example for the rest of the team. This employee may be using "demonstrated busyness" as a proxy for productivity. Absent clear, small goals that clearly connect to the larger organizational goal, this person may be using what seems like a reasonable measurement. Your responsibility as a manager is to clearly state clear goals that clearly advance the larger needs of the organization. Watch her walk out the door with nothing more than a purse and car keys at 5 p.m. three days a week, or buy her a cup of coffee and bagel on Monday morning if you don't hear from her over the weekend. Reward small goals that support the larger goal rather than let her try to guess what counts.

These small goals can keep your staff focused and progressing toward what can seem like an abstract or remote goal. It's these small goals that will make the big one reachable – or not. Think about the FitBit or other apps that track how many steps you take and even share them on social media. "Get healthy" is a laudable but daunting goal, but "take 10,000 steps a day" is doable and measurable, and we all know the lengths we will go to in order to hit that number. As a manager you can set these small goals and hold staff to them, and you can also set them for yourself and hold yourself to them.

When I was a Chief of Staff and campaign manager in the House of Representatives the big goal was easy to identify: 14 months from when I was hired my boss had to get one more vote than the other guy in the election. Along the way I set up little targets that advanced that goal – I aimed for an average of a press clip a day, for example, because in elections press attention tends to translate into voter attention. No one set that goal, and I'm not sure I shared it with anyone, but it was one that kept me on track and focused every day. At another organization I set a goal of turning off my smart phone at 8 p.m. and not turning it back on until I got to my desk the next morning. I told my staff this goal and suggested they set a similar one. With few exceptions, I stuck to my goal which made it easier for my direct reports to do the same. This kept them rested and at their best, rather than just frantically doing stuff to demonstrate to me (and themselves) they were good employees.

## Locker Room Notes for Managers

Make sure you are measuring and rewarding the right things.

Set interim goals for your direct reports that are both measurable and meaningful.

Set interim goals for yourself and measure your own progress against them.

Avoid the urge to measure what's convenient solely because it's convenient.

## Locker Room Notes for Staff

Set personal goals that advance the organization's mission and track your progress toward those goals.

Work with your supervisor to set professional goals that both advance the organizational mission and that are measurable.

Avoid the urge to measure what's convenient solely because it's convenient.

## Endnotes

1. A reminder that in soccer a tackle is taking the ball from another player, not dragging the other player down.

## Chapter 11

# The Limits of Under-Dogdem and Over-Dogdem

Being the scrappy underdog can get your players and staff to over-perform. But remaining the underdog is exhausting, unsustainable, and ultimately a self-fulfilling prophesy. Players and staff who think they are better than they are can do great things in the short term, but a single setback can be equally demoralizing.

*At the top levels of competition, there is little difference in skill between players. Obviously, the world-class players such as Lionel Messi and Cristiano Ronaldo are almost always noticeable, but those players are few and far between. The real difference between players at the top levels is not necessarily physical, but it is more psychological in nature. The difference in skill among the top ranked college teams is relatively nominal; rather, the difference is primarily psychological. You have to think like a winner. That requires the requisite levels of psychological preparation, hard work, confidence, but also humility -- respecting your opponent.*
Antonio Soave, Former Kansas Secretary of Commerce, Chairman and CEO of Capistrano Global Advisory Services, former head coach at Ave Maria University in Florida and Franciscan University of Steubenville in Ohio, and former semi-professional player

*You may have heard the phrase, 'Fake it 'til you make it.' I prefer to say 'Act as if.' Act as if you already have what you want, and the chances are you'll get it. Life is a self-fulfilling prophecy, and with the right attitude and determination, you'll start to get what you*

*want. It might not happen overnight, but you'll get there.*
Vince Stanzione "The Millionaire Dropout"

Over the course of about 10 days I had two versions of the same conversation, one with a soccer coach and the other with a friend who is the executive director of an international organization. The conversations went something like this: Being the scrappy underdog can motivate staff and get people to perform beyond their own expectations in the short term, but being the underdog who knows he isn't as good as others is exhausting and risks ensuring eventual failure.

About two-thirds of the way through a long season an underdog team was beginning to fade. All season they had been described by the press and fans as underdogs who over achieved. Players read the paper, knew whether or not they were well-paid international stars, and believed the underdog label. When the team had a few losses they began to act as if things were finally going as they should – the team started to meet the expectations others had of them. Rather than continuing to exceed those expectations they began to perform as they thought everyone expected them to, and as they expected themselves to, and they began to lose. It is exhausting getting up every day believing you have to work harder than anyone else just to keep up. Being told you're not as good as everyone else but if you work really hard you can get lucky, takes a lot out of a person both physically and emotionally. Perpetual underdog status is also unsustainable because your own assumption of your own failure is baked into your success. You start from the premise that you are supposed to lose. As a result, when you do lose you think "I knew this was coming, we're not good enough and it's finally showing." Players who expect to lose, tend to lose.

I've played a lot of soccer. I've been on pretty bad teams and pretty good teams and in pickup games where I'm among the best on the field and among the worst of the field. Whenever

I step onto the field I do my best when I assume that I'm good enough to be there. If I assume I can get to every ball, win every tackle, and complete every pass I am more likely to fight for every ball, go into tackles rather than just let the person go by, and look for good passes rather than just boot the ball and hope for the best. Of course I'm not first to a lot of balls, get beaten a lot, and miss a lot of passes, but so does everyone and at least I'm giving it a shot which makes me a better player.

The executive director I mentioned at the beginning, who I will call Julia, had been with the organization a long time. She moved up through the ranks to run the DC office and eventually the entire organization. She raised the organization's profile and impact, taking it from a respected scrappy over-achieving group to a leading force in the field. Over coffee she said that an unexpected challenge was getting her staff to embrace their new role as Goliath rather than David. She said that they still carried themselves as if they were perpetual outsiders doomed to fail, and were surprised to be invited to big meetings and otherwise treated as a legitimate force. Julia wanted the staff to embrace an assumption of success. She wanted them to act as if they were not invited to the meeting, then the meeting was not important by definition. The organization was winning because it was good and it was right, not because it was plucky and lucky, and she needed her staff to act as such. Julia was concerned that if her staff did not make this shift at the first sign of trouble or failure the staff would not work as hard and not do as well.

Assuming the role of the underdog can be a great short-term motivator and it can be fun and rewarding watching someone's inner David come out when facing a Goliath. But that can only be a short-term tactic, not a long-term strategy. David is always smaller and weaker; he got headlines for pulling off the unexpected against an overconfident and stronger opponent; the story is compelling because Goliath usually won and David usually lost. My greatest successes have come when teams and organizations of which I have been a part knew their strengths and weaknesses, and assumed inevitable victory. We figured out where we were better than our opposition or competition and ran hard at that strength – we might have been smaller but we figured exactly where to throw the rock. The real lesson of David and Goliath might be that smart and agile beats big and slow. If you figure out where and how you are likely to win, and if you assume you deserve to succeed, your staff will be more resilient. They will take setbacks as minor bumps to be solved or simply rolled over on the road to success rather than as proof that they are not as good and thus reasons to pack it in.

> *Customer: Hi, do you have the song "I Just Called To Say I Love You?" It's for my daughter's birthday.*
> *Barry: Yea we have it.*
> *Customer: Great, Great, can I have it?*
> *Barry: No, no, you can't.*
> *Customer: Why not?*
> *Barry: Well, it's sentimental tacky crap. Do we look like the kind of store that sells "I Just Called to Say I Love You?" Go to the mall.*
> High Fidelity

An element of assuming underdog status that shows up in advocacy organizations more than on the soccer field is that for some failure is proof of purity or righteousness. This is the record store staff in High Fidelity – failure is evidence of moral superiority and as a result success raises questions about moral failure. Having one's ideas rejected by one's superiors becomes evidence of a manager's failings and the superiority of junior staff because the managers "just don't get it." Junior staff whose ideas are adopted can quickly earn the resentment of others for selling out or sucking up.

Underdogism is ultimately a losing approach in part because of the psychic energy it takes to go to work every day believing you aren't as good as your colleagues or competitors. It fails in part because failure becomes a self-fulfilling prophesy. Underdogism also burns people out, which itself can help create the failure that leads to the downward spiral. Those who have confidence that they will succeed know they can take time to read outside of work, take pottery classes, or spend a few days at an adult soccer camp. As a result, these employees are more likely to be more productive, more creative, and thus more successful. The actions that follow assumed success helped create that success, just as the attitudes do.

## Locker Room Notes for Managers

When you have a project or assignment that seems too big use it as an opportunity to get them to step into roles you know they can fill; encourage them to stretch because you know they can, not because you need them to pull off the impossible.

Tell your staff that they were hired because they can succeed, do not tell them they were hired because they are scrappy outsiders or because they are the best ever.

## Locker Room Notes for Staff

Be realistic about your strengths and weaknesses, and believe you can find a way to win with that mix.

Take failure (to advance, to get your idea heard, etc.) as a bump to learn from, not as proof that either the idea, product, or service is bad or that customers and decision makers are stupid.

Do not assume that because you are successful today that you are better than objective analysis would demonstrate.

# Chapter 12

# Failure and Fame are Fleeting

Soccer players do not dwell on the last pass or play, regardless of how good or bad it was. A good shot does not mean the next shot will be good, and a bad pass does not mean the next pass will be bad. The best players figure out what went right or wrong and adjust as needed. The best managers and staff learn from individual successes and mistakes, and never confuse one good or bad action for a good or bad career.

> *The vital traits for a soccer goalkeeper are good hands, quick feet and a short memory. Concede a goal, forget it. The match marches on.*
> Steve Goff, "After rough Premier League season, Brad Guzan aims for smooth transition at Copa America"

> *I can't recall a single thing I learned from winning.*
> Mary Harvey, goalkeeper on US Women's 1991 World Cup winning team

One successful action does not mean more successes will necessarily follow. Success may improve your confidence, and if you try to learn why you were successful you may be more likely to be successful again, but the act of succeeding does not automatically result in more successes. In many ways this is the flip side of the risk of a constant underdog attitude. Restauranteur and former professional soccer player Ari Gedjenson points out that players who are performing above their talent level, and mistake this surge in skill for their baseline ability, may not be able to recover when their true talent level is revealed. It is one thing to believe you're not that good, perform well, and then have your initial belief confirmed. It is quite another to think you're great only to find out you're not – that can be much more difficult for players and teams to recover from.

But just as one success does not mean future success will follow, one failure does not make someone an underdog finally performing to his expected low level.

One of the first lessons that professional athletes learn is to focus on one play at a time. Don't think about the game, or your role in the large arch of 90 minutes of play or the many months of the season. Think about receiving the next pass and getting the ball under control. Then pass the ball. Then move. Your last pass and your next move are not this pass and this move. If your most recent pass was errant that does not mean your next one will be, and if your last pass was perfect that does not mean the rest of your passes in the game will be perfect. Passes happen one at a time. Players do not have good or bad games, they have good or bad plays. The plays may add up to good or bad games, but plays happen one at a time.

*It is easy to get caught up in thinking about mistakes you have made in the past. A bad pass in the opening minutes of a game can have a significant effect on the rest of the game, if you let it.*

*Worrying about a mistake you've made will not correct it and will cause you to lose your focus for the remainder of the competition. Even though you have made a bad pass, the game is not over and you still have the chance to do well and make an impact. It takes a mentally tough player to be able to regain composure and focus after a bad touch or missed opportunity.*

How do you (or your soccer players) respond to mistakes? Soccer Psychology Tips

Professional players make tons of mistakes. Most mistakes are passing being a little too long or short, shots being a little too high or too wide, or defensive positioning a little off or tackles a little mistimed. Sometimes the errors are laughable. Every season there are a few videos of top professionals miskicking the ball so badly it not only goes wide of the goal but manages to somehow go out of bounds on the sidelines, 20 or more yards from the target. Every weekend, world class forwards try to kick balls and miss them entirely. Championship goalkeepers let the ball go through their legs. Players sometimes trip over their own feet. These mistakes get mocked by commentators and result in groans from the fans (or laughter, depending on which team they're rooting for), and get played endlessly on TV and online. But the players keep on playing. They go after the person they turned the ball over to, hustle back to defend when their shot gets blocked, and they chase down the forward who dribbled past them. A goalkeeper who kicks the ball to an onrushing forward to give up a goal in the opening minute of a World Cup qualifying game keeps making saves and solid clearances for the rest of the match.[1]

In pickup and rec league soccer the errors are more common and more egregious, though mercifully there is rarely anyone watching. The forward who sends a shot over the crossbar, or even over crossbar and over the fence into the street, won't hesitate to take the next shot. Players may talk after a mistake to sort out miscommunication, and you will often see a player who has scuffed a shot examining the field for holes or hills, but all of them get on with the next play. Similarly a player who makes a great pass or tackle, or scores a terrific goal, keeps going into the next pass, tackle, and shot.

In soccer a good pass or defensive play is sometimes greeted with "great pass" or "nice d(efense)" but no one stops because by the time the compliment is shouted the next play is already over. Similarly, if someone makes a mistake there are occasional shouts of "bad luck," sometimes the person who made the mistake will hold up their hand to take ownership of the error, or a teammate will applaud the effort even if it didn't pan out. Regardless, play goes on, the next pass is attempted, and the next tackle tried. Professional soccer players have epic goal celebrations, but if time is short they run to get the ball out of the net and get on with the game. In rec league or pickup games most of the celebrations are for show or goofing off, no one takes them too seriously.

Failure to get on with the game can result in failure on the field. If you think you're that good because you just completed a terrific pass or great defensive move, or scored a pretty goal (golazo in soccer-speak), then you might not reflect on what made your success – was it your concentration? Your positioning? Was it because someone on the other team made a mistake? Was it a bump on the field or dumb luck? If you do not know why you were successful you are less likely to be successful again. And let's face it, if you act like you're all that and a massive transfer fee you will come off like a jerk because you're acting like a jerk. If you're a jerk on the field people won't want to get you the ball or want you on the team. If you're constantly evaluating your own success you're likely to remain humble and that is a good thing to be because you will keep getting better (and being humble is a good thing to be in general, regardless of any benefits).

*Losing never lasts very long.*
Len Oliver, writer and consultant, National Soccer Hall of Fame, former professional player and member of the US Olympic Team

Failure to move on from a mistake can be worse. One immediate reaction to a mistake can be to hang your head, kick the ground, or give up. Those all make the situation worse – sometimes much worse. If you make a bad pass and the ball goes to an opponent, you need to immediately put yourself in a position to win the ball back. If you have the ball taken from you, you need to fight to get it back. If someone runs by you with the ball, chase them. One recent Sunday a teammate playing center-back – a typically solid player and terrific guy – waited too long to decide what to do with the ball and ultimately passed it to an onrushing forward for the other team, who promptly and easily scored. The first mistake my teammate made was waiting too long to decide what to do and the second mistake was giving the ball away. But neither mistake needed to be fatal – the fatal mistake was giving up. After his bad pass, my teammate hung his head and gave up as the opponent ran by him with the ball. The first two mistakes would have been quickly forgotten, but the mistake of giving up was of a different order of magnitude and remained part of the sideline chatter for the rest of the game.

Right before halftime in the final game of the 1991 Women's World Cup the US goalkeeper, Mary Harvey, came out to punch away a ball but hit her own player instead and gave up a tying goal. The team headed into the locker room at 1-1 rather than 1-0. The learning moment for Harvey was completely letting go of what had happened, focusing instead on what she did next. Harvey went out for the second half focused on the remaining 45 minutes and the US went on to win 2-1.

If you do not quickly figure out what went wrong and make any needed adjustment you will be afraid to try the pass, shot, or tackle again, removing an important tool from your team. If the opposition knows you are afraid to try a long pass they won't bother to guard against it and will put a defender somewhere else. If the opposition knows you're afraid to shoot the ball they won't bother covering you in the attack, freeing up their defenders to guard everyone else. You need to keep trying the shot, keep trying the pass, and keep defending. If you're not sure what went wrong or how to improve, ask. If you figured out what went wrong and cannot improve, work with your teammates to compensate. If you cannot hit the long pass, ask your teammates to come closer or provide other options. If the guy you are defending is faster than you either drop back so you don't have to chase him or switch positions with someone on your team who has the wheels. But keep playing. Try, learn, repeat.

*Failure is not particularly an option for me, but sometimes it becomes a reality. It knocks you down, and you have to go on and get stronger because of it.*
Danny Karbassiyoon, Co-Founder and Product Lead, SWOL/ Fury90, former Arsenal player

I got more than 29,000,000 results when I searched "learning from business failure" on Google in January 2016. Apparently people fail a lot and want to know how to make that failure a good thing. It is also fair to say that not only do people fail a lot but they also fail to turn that failure into success.

Some of that is no doubt because the Failure is Good industry focuses on Big Failure, the serial entrepreneur who invented five terrible apps before hitting on the thing that paid for his boat, or James Dyson bragging that he had more than 5,000 failed prototypes before the model for the design that would make him rich. When business publications talk about failure they mean it with a capital F, not the botched presentation or typo in the annual report sort of failure but the collapse of a company sort of failure. This is the equivalent of a star forward sending a penalty kick sailing into the stands and costing his team the World Cup, as legendary Italian player Roberto Baggio did in the final against Brazil in 1994.

The victory industry is the same, celebrating and examining big victories in business or sports, lessons from people who dominated their sport or upended an industry. But most of us will never be Diego Maradona scoring an unbelievable goal against England in the 1986 World Cup (not the "hand of God" goal, the other one).

Most of us, most of the time, make far less memorable mistakes and have far fewer memorable victories. Not many of us invented an industry in our garage or launched a revolutionary record label in our dorm room. Most of our mistakes are the equivalent of scoring an own-goal in a pickup or rec leagues game, or posting something on social media that we should not have posted. In the moment the embarrassment and anxiety of the failure can be excruciating, and the thrill of getting a Board of Directors to applaud a presentation can be exhilarating. The size of the failure and success makes the lesson no less important. A great event or presentation is great, but don't do a victory dance and certainly don't expect the next one to automatically go as well. Figure out what went right and start working on the next one. A botched event or presentation is just that, a single botched event. Figure out what went wrong, adjust as appropriate, and move on to the next task.

I once worked in a large building that had several interior atriums and terrible acoustics, sound would echo up and around and back again. I managed to schedule a high profile event in one of the atriums at the same time as an event in another atrium – not necessarily a big deal, except that my event was a serious talk with serious and high-profile people, and the other event was a gathering of high school students. As soon as the glitch became clear I let the folks who needed to know that there could be some unexpected noise, worked with staff to decrease the chances the events would get in each other's way, and attended my event. There were some moments of ill-timed applause from one area echoing into the next, but otherwise everything was fine and both events went well. The people responsible for the scheduling glitch gathered after the events, figured out how to prevent a similar conflict from happening in the future, and got on with the next task. No one's job was threatened, there wasn't a lot of blame-casting, and the mistake wasn't repeated.

*Crisis is good for you. Be happy when your organisation is in crisis, because that will be for sure the moment to do real things and to develop real changes.*
Alex Aranzábal Mínguez, Partner AYA – Aguirre y Aranzabal and former President of SD Eibar in La Liga

Someone who worked for one of my direct reports once organized an event and asked me to give the welcoming remarks. The event was OK from the perspective of the participants, but from where I sat it was a mess. The packets he handed out were incomplete and what was in them was not in the order they would be used (for example not all of the speakers' bios were in the packets. I know because mine was among those missing). The point of the day wasn't made clear to the participants. The tie to our organization wasn't made clear either. The event was a mess. I let his boss (who reported to me) know, let her know that I wasn't mad because the event itself didn't matter that much and was fine, and that I wanted to talk to the staffer the next day about how the event went from his perspective and how he would change it for next year. I could have just told his boss I would be doing these things – the org chart gave me that authority – but such assertions of power tend to do more harm than good; better to respectfully ask than simply assert and I was a member of her team following her lead in that moment. The junior staff member and I sat down, and I asked how he thought it went. His view was different than mine, so I coached him through it – how about this? How about that? Where did this fit? What about that opportunity? He saw the mistakes and we talked about how he would correct them, and I immediately told him I looked forward to giving the welcome at the event next year and that I was sure he would do a great job. We talked about how he could improve and I left him in charge; we got on with the game. The next year he ran the event, and, as expected, it was better.

## Locker Room Notes for Managers

When a member of your staff makes a mistake or succeeds, identify the elements that went into that mistake or success and help the staff member avoid or repeat those elements in the future – focus on what led to the outcome, not the outcome itself.

Keep individual errors and victories in context – no one outcome defines a career or person.

## Locker Room Notes for Staff

After a mistake or victory identify the elements that led to that mistake or success; figure out how to adjust for the errors or repeat the success, and then forget about the event itself.

Remember that no one is the worst or best thing they have ever done.

## Endnotes

1. This happened in a World Cup qualifying game between the US and Mexico in 1997, the game ended in a 2-2 tie.

## Chapter 13

# Don't Just Do Something, Sit There

The best soccer players remain calm under pressure and know when to try to take the ball and when to just contain an opponent, when to shoot and when to hold onto the ball, and when to pass and when to knock the ball out of bounds. The best managers and staff similarly know when a situation requires immediate action, when a situation requires attention, and what can be ignored.

> *Skillful players make the right decisions at the right time, and know how and what the right thing to do is in every game scenario.*
> The Away End Blog "Skill is decision making, not scissors"

> *Don't just do something – sit there.*
> Boston political consultant Michael Goldman

We all love to watch soccer players do amazing tricks. We love the step-overs, Cruyff turns, and juggling (what the English call "keepy uppy," which is both a more descriptive and more fun term for bouncing the ball in the air with your feet or head). Those skills are fun to watch, and at the top level everyone can do some of it. If you are good at something, and especially if that something is flashy, you tend to do it a lot. The most skilled soccer players are those who know when to use which skills, many of which look boring or may not even be noticed at all. Games change as players get tired, the field gets wetter or more snow covered, as the sun shifts putting parts of the field in shadow or glare, as players get substituted, as the opponent adjusts its system, and on and on. Having a trick up your sleeve is great, but knowing when to use that trick and when to defer to a teammate's sleeve, is better.

The same holds true for offices and organizations. You have to be good at what you do and you need tricks up your sleeve. That could be social media, design, commodities futures, or whatever – there is something you do well enough that people pay you to do it. But if you don't see how your skill, your flair, fits the larger system you will only ever be that skill person. If you use your own single skill in every situation, you risk becoming a liability. You are the hammer for whom the world is made up of nails. If you know when to use your skill and when to defer to others, if you have good judgment, you will be put in charge of projects being done by those with specific skills.

*Research published in the Journal of Sport and Exercise Psychology found that of 39 players tested, the more experienced footballers were able to suppress the urge to act instinctively, making them less susceptible to feints or tricks from their opponents. Brunel's study reinforces the view held by one of the greatest players of all time – Johan Cruyff, who said that football is a game you play with your brain.*
Chris Murphy, "Mind over matter: Soccer's bid to train the brain"

Defenders often shout "don't dive in," "stand him up," or "contain." This means stand between the player with the ball and the goal. Slow the play down and let your teammates get in position to help. Don't try to take the ball from him ("diving in") or try to force him one way or another ("stand him up," "contain"). Just try to prevent the guy with the ball from doing anything, limit his options and be in the way. In other words, don't just do something – sit there.

The step overs and feints and shimmies and such are attempts by the player with the ball to get the defender to make a move, so the guy with the ball can move around him. As a defender it can be hard not to take the bait. You see an opening and want to seize it, or you're tired so you lunge, or you get caught in the moment and you chase. The problem is that the person with the ball knows what he wants to do with it, so will always be a fraction of a second ahead; if he shifts his shoulders left and touches the ball ever so slightly in that direction, it could be a chance for you to steal it or it could be his chance to get you to commit while he goes the other way. The best players are able to make calm decisions even under immense pressure and when tired. They keep a clear focus on the task: prevent the player with the ball from getting past or shooting and act to ensure they accomplish that task. The best defenders don't watch an opponent's shoulders or hips – the best defenders resist the urge to do something and keep their eyes on the ball.

*Training in soccer is about practicing decision making.*
Ben Olsen, DC United Head Coach and former Olympic and World Cup player

Sometimes in soccer the threat comes from an entire team or from a player without the ball. Teams can pass the ball around and players can run into corners or into empty space. Teams can dominate possession and deny an opponent many opportunities. It is tempting to chase the running players and disrupt the passing – after all, the more the other team has the ball the more time they have to score, and the less time your team has the ball the fewer scoring opportunities your team can create. But the point of soccer isn't passing or running, the point is goals. As long as the passing is around midfield, side to side, or backward then it really doesn't matter. If the players running into space are running into space where it is hard to shoot from, then let them be – "don't chase" in soccer-speak. In the face of teams that like to pass a lot and run a lot, smart teams stay organized and disciplined, wait for the opponent to make a mistake, and strike quickly on a counter-attack. While teams that pass and run without making progress are expending energy not advancing their goal, the best opponents sit and wait for their moment to strike. Think of Indiana Jones coming up against the overly skilled, prepared and confident swordsman in the market, and simply shooting him.

Some of the best professional advice I ever got was from Michael Goldman, a political consultant and a professor of mine at Emerson College: Don't just do something – sit there.

There are two types of professional situations to which we may feel compelled to respond – attacks on the company and movements in the market. When something happens at your organization or in your field, the instinct to do something can be nearly overwhelming. If your company or industry is being attacked in social media or the press the first instinct can be to respond immediately – somebody said something so we must say something back! If everyone in your industry is rushing in one direction the temptation to rush in with them is powerful.

Sometimes getting caught in that moment is a good thing. There are times when an attack calls for an immediate and overwhelming response. Market opportunities do not often hang around and wait for you to be completely comfortable with a course of action. But sometimes the attack is less than it seems or the result of the attack may not matter. Sometimes the market is wrong.

Several years ago a friend who was vice president of communications of a national organization called for my take on an issue. A publication had mentioned the organization in a story about places where interns are not treated well, and several senior staff said that the organization should immediately respond to the story. Her view was that no one outside the organization even noticed the story, and if they did it wasn't clear what negative impact it would have – there was no reason to worry. On the other hand, responding could raise the profile of the attack, and would also divert scarce staff resources from other priorities. After asking what the worst possible outcome would be from ignoring the piece and letting the attack stand (fewer people would apply to be interns) I agreed with her. Because time and money are finite, and anything done to respond to the attack would divert attention from other more important work, any effort put into responding would be worse than the worst case scenario from not responding.

Ignoring the external herd can often be more important. The premise of the best-selling book and Academy Award winning film about the housing collapse "The Big Short" is that everyone leapt but nobody looked. A handful of people made a lot of money because they didn't dive in, they didn't just do something. They figured out the difference between flashy moves and what was actually going to happen. A lot of other people fell for the flash that did not mean anything and lost incredible sums of money. The best business leaders figure out how to keep an eye on their goal, separate the flash from the actual action, and act on the action. To steal the title of Nate Silver's 2012 book on why most predictions are wrong, the best business leaders know how to tell the signal from the noise.[1]

Determining whether or not to "just do something" because of threats or opportunities requires a clear focus on the organization's goals and an honest assessment of both what the range of outcomes of the threat or opportunity could be, what it would take to counter those threats or seize those opportunities, and honest weighting of the costs and benefits. The instinct to "just do something" within an organization can be as strong. An errant email, frustrating meeting, or rumors about shakeups, can cause panic and make staff want to dive in – with more meetings, petitions, more rumors, and more. The best staff keep a clear eye on the goal and focus on that.

## Locker Room Notes for Managers

Before acting on a threat or opportunity ask your staff for honest assessments of the threats and opportunities, the costs or responding, and what will not happen as a result of responding.

Before acting or directing your staff, determine how great the threat is to the organization's goal; if the threat does not impact the goal, and if the benefit is to someone else's goal, leave it alone.

## Locker Room Notes for Staff

Do not dive into threats or opportunities.

Before acting on a threat or opportunity ask "what's the best or worst that could happen?" "what would it take to respond?" and "will the net benefit of acting outweigh the benefit of not-acting?"

## Chapter 14

# Get Fit along the Way

We get good at something by making a plan, doing it, making mistakes, making adjustments, and doing it again. This is true on the field and in the office.

> *The Leicester fans I meet in the street tell me they are dreaming. But I say to them, 'Okay, you dream for us. We do not dream. We simply work hard.'*
> Claudio Ranieri, manager of the Leicester City Football Club that won the English title in 2016 in spite of being 5,000 – 1 underdogs "We Do Not Dream"

> *You have to train; training is about making habits.*
> Kajeet CEO Daniel Neal on a parallel between soccer success and business success

My father tells the story about a bicyclist he met at a scenic overlook in Maine. My dad was driving back from a camping trip and pulled over to stretch his legs and take in the view. He saw a guy on a fully equipped bicycle and asked where he had biked from. "California," the rider said. Appropriately impressed, my dad asked how he trained for the 3,000 mile journey. "I got fit along the way" was the reply. The way you prepare your body to pedal from the Pacific Ocean to the Atlantic Ocean is to get on your bike and start peddling. The rider was successful because he worked at being successful as he worked. The first day was hard. He made some adjustments and got a little stronger, and the second day was easier. He made a few more adjustments and got a little stronger, and the third day was easier. By the time he made it to Maine his body knew what to do and he had done it. There was no complex training regime or secret psychological ritual – the guy got on his bike and headed east until he ran out of land. One can imagine a similar conversation taking place in Ohio – "where are you going?" "I'm riding from California to Maine." "How did you train for that?" "By riding from California to Ohio."

In soccer getting fit along the way means lots of touches on the ball and playing a lot of games. Players practice by passing to each other, dribbling around cones, knocking a ball against a wall, and rolling the ball around their feet. The pros do the same drills as your daughter's high school team. It is not about complexity, it is about repetition and practice. The more touches you have in practice or on your own the better you get and the easier the touches will come in the game. The more games you play the better you are at playing in games. Soccer players don't know how they made a particular pass or dribbled past a particular player, any more than the bicyclist knew what technique he used to cross Ohio. They did what they did until it worked.

A common refrain in any sport is "practice like you play." The best players and the best teams get ready for games and game situations by running through game situations and playing games. You successfully defend against corner kicks in games by defending against them in practice. You get good at the give-and-go by endlessly giving and going. The best players in the world did not start that way. When they started they were probably pretty bad. There was a time, if only briefly, when any one of us could have beaten the great Lionel Messi. Messi got to be Messi in part by practicing, by playing, and by relentlessly working on skills that he needs to succeed in games.

Over the years I have advised a lot of organizations of all shapes and sizes that want to make a change. These organizations are rightly concerned about getting the changes right. A challenge is that no new effort is perfect on the first try and no one is perfect at the new role on the first day. New approaches and new skills take practice. A company or organization cannot start out by being good at something, it has to get good at something.

A medium-sized national organization that was well-respected for its research but was a bit under the radar asked a group of us to help it raise its profile and become more effective. We sat down with the organization's leadership and led multi-day planning sessions with butcher paper and colored markers. Based on that work we drafted a plan to achieve their goals. The organization was hesitant – what if it wasn't the right path? What if they didn't have the right staff? What about what would go wrong? All of those are reasonable concerns. So I told the story of my father meeting the bicyclist in Maine. I said that their fears were justified and that they would make mistakes. Some of the staff might thrive in the new approach, but some might have to be let go. The organization would miss opportunities and things would go wrong. Becoming the new organization would be hard. But change would get easier as they kept changing. They would identify and correct their mistakes. Some staff would leave or would need to be let go, and they would be replaced by others more suited to the tasks at hand. The organization, like the intrepid biker, would get fit along the way. The organization took the chance. They initially used the firm at which I was working for help with press, online, organizing, and strategy. As the organization got better at the tasks it shed our services the way one takes training wheels off a bicycle. Eventually the organization cut us off entirely, which we saw as a win for us and them. Several years later I happened to be talking to the organization's executive director and she said she continues to rely on the metaphor of "getting fit along the way" to help her organization continue to grow and succeed. Actions that were once difficult tasks had become habits, and she was both more prepared to take on new challenges and less afraid of making mistakes as she did so.

When I was at the Food and Drug Administration, the

Commissioner noted that the FDA did not have a coordinated, strategic, outreach program to academic medical centers, or AMCs. AMCs are increasingly complex networks of medical schools, hospitals, schools of public health, big industry, and small entrepreneurs. The work at AMCs drives health care innovation and delivery. The FDA ought to be in regular contact with these centers to help steer research along the right track, to learn from the work being done, and to be a partner in protecting and promoting public health. With the help of a lot of colleagues, I pulled together all the existing FDA/AMC relationships I could find. I constructed a spread sheet that listed all the nation's medical schools and ranked the order in which to visit them based on how many were in an area, if we already had invitations to visit them, companies in the area, and so forth. The Commissioner and I went back and forth several times over several weeks to identify the best approach. Then, knowing we would make mistakes and that the unexpected would happen, we started. We picked a first stop – in this case expanding an already planned speech at the medical school at Yale University – and went. In going we figured out glitches in scheduling and travel, and planned the next trip. And then the next. And the next. We hit eight states between mid-October and early December (seven of those states in four weeks). The trips included more than 30 meetings, a dozen speeches, and a tour of an FDA field office. We planned, prepared, and went. Adjusted our plans, prepared more, and went again.

The lesson for managers and staff is to have a clear goal – "bike from California to Maine," "accurately pass the ball," "become a trusted advocacy organization," "build relationships with stakeholders" – and work on the skills needed to achieve that goal. As a manager who wants to create a "total football" organization those skills could include regularly asking staff how what they are working on at the moment relates to the work being done by their colleagues to advance the organization's goals. It could mean thinking deliberately about how the work of one group could be used by another group within the organization to advance organizational goals, or thinking about what support that group needs to succeed.

*Practice like you play. Don't just show up at meetings, you have to prepare for them. Managing a project is like the preparation and training before a game, delivering the final product is like the match itself. Each meeting your product should be getting better and you owe it to your team to be prepared and be the best you can be from the beginning of the project to the end.*
Neil Richardson, Founder Emergent Action, co-author of *Preparing for a World that Doesn't Exist – Yet*, former professional soccer player Richmond Kickers

For example, might current or potential customers want to hear about the good work being done by the research teams? Can professional accolades for your staff be used by human resources to help recruit top talent to the firm? Can sales growth be used to encourage marketing to keep generating good ideas? Think about the specific steps needed to achieve your goals, and work on those steps. And keep working on them. Know that you will start by exerting a lot of effort and making a lot of mistakes, and that eventually the task will be easier and you'll be better at it, and it will become a habit. Keep kicking the ball, keep peddling east.

Similarly, you should practice presentations as if you were giving the presentation. If you expect hard questions during a pitch, practice answering hard questions ahead of time. If the room in which you will be speaking is cavernous and has poor acoustics, find a place that's big and carries sound poorly to practice. If you have to drive a visiting executive or VIP around, practice the route ahead of time, ideally at the same time of day to account for traffic, sun glare, and roads that may only be open (or closed) during rush hour. By the time you do something that matters, when it matters, you should have already done it as if it mattered.

## Locker Room Notes for Managers

Focus on staff improvement toward a goal.

Reward improvement along the way to the goal. Any corrective action should be that which makes the goal more achievable. Don't worry if your staff doesn't do everything perfectly, instead focus on your team doing everything better.

## Locker Room Notes for Staff

Make every effort your best effort.

Don't worry about being perfect, focus on getting better.

Chapter 15

# Referees Keep the Game Going

Good referees and good managers know their role is to keep things going.

*The ref is challenged and respected – in soccer there is no instant replay, no technology aiding/deciding the 'answer' to a call\*, and this creates ambiguity/grey areas for refs and coaches/players alike to challenge calls (informally; unlike football where there are formal channels to challenge calls), express anger and disgust towards a call, and yet at the same time, have complete and total respect for the job that needs to be done and the person that has been selected to do that job – this is a great example of that dynamic – healthy banter, mix between challenging authority and respecting it, is a key lesson to apply in business (necessary to constantly push into the grey space).*
Ashley Amin, former NCAA Division I soccer player at The George Washington University and social entrepreneur

\*Some technology is being introduced in some leagues and for some decisions, but by and large adjudication is done on the fly with no review.

*[A] US President, like a good referee, works to facilitate a game that is neither 'too tight' nor 'too soft.' Like Baby Bear's porridge, he or she wants a game that is 'just right,' so that the animal spirits of the free market, combined with the creative genius of entrepreneurs, can work their magic.*
James Marshall Crotty, "Like a Good Referee, the Next US President Should Be Measured, Courageous, and Decidedly Not the Story"

We often think of referees as people whose primary responsibility is to enforce the rules and stop the play. In most sports, the referee intervenes when there is an infraction. He blows the whistle, punishes the offender, and then restarts the action. But in soccer the referee's job is to keep the play going in ways that are fair and that keep the players safe. A good soccer referee helps the game go.

Soccer referees are given the leeway to enforce the spirit of the laws of the game rather than the specifics of a particular law. This can mean letting some infractions go and adjusting the punishment to fit the situation and player. If a ref sees a foul, he may wait to see if the team that was fouled would be more hurt by stopping the play than by letting it continue; if the player fouled continues on, the ref lets it go, he "plays the advantage." When play eventually stops because a ball goes out of bounds the ref may go back to the player who committed the foul and talk to him – let him know the ref saw the infraction and not to do it again, or give him a yellow (or even red) card after the fact[2] – but in the moment the play goes on because the point of the game is the game, not its laws. Rec league referees often adjust their approach to the skill level of the players, allowing all sorts of technical infractions to go unpunished as long as they are not too egregious.

In pickup soccer the rules are even more fungible – if a ball goes out of bounds a little the other team may shout "play on" to keep the play moving rather than stop everything just to start it again. The point of pickup is to play, and every break in play goes against that point. This is especially true if the player is new or the teams uneven – a newer player will be given more leeway, and a team that is doing much worse will be given a few breaks to keep things fun and interesting.

Referees in soccer are also given leeway to interpret the laws in ways that are fair and protect the players. In 1996 the Laws of the Game were re-written and "intent" was largely removed

– an elbow to the head is a foul, whether or not the ref thinks it was intentional or accidental. But referees at the top level still use their judgment in handing out more severe punishments like yellow or red cards. Most players most of the time are not allowed to touch the ball with their arms or hands, but referees often don't call hand balls if they think the player could not do anything about it, or if the players arm was against his body and the ball happened to hit the arm rather than the player's side. Refs constantly make judgment calls to keep the play going and the players safe.

In rec league soccer good refs will adjust to both the level of the game and level of play. Sometimes that may mean blowing the whistle more often to keep everyone safe, and sometimes less often because casual players make more innocent mistakes (in my experience, rec league referees allow far less physical play than the pros in an effort to keep everyone as injury-free as possible, but call fewer handballs because we casual players flail around a lot more than the pros do). The point of a rec league game is to not get hurt, win, and have fun. A good ref keeps the game going in ways that prevent injury, give both teams a fair chance of winning, and keep tensions down. That may, or may not, mean blowing the whistle with every infraction. As former rec league ref Dave Tyahla puts it, the goal of the ref is to use his whistle as little as possible.

Players and refs at all levels talk to each other (with "talk to" sometimes being a euphemism for "yell at," "plead with," and "publicly question the lineage and optical qualities of"). Players ask for clarifications of calls, encourage the ref to keep an eye on certain players, and of course players complain bitterly in the moment. Good refs also talk to players, explaining why a foul was or was not called, cautioning them to calm down, and otherwise keep them on track to keep the game moving. The ref's word is final, but is not handed down from an isolated position.

And of course referees sometimes get it wrong. Over 90

minutes of soccer players and officials make mistakes. They have good calls and bad calls, and good games and bad games. Like players, they work on getting better and know that they will never be perfect. All players and refs can hope is that over the course of a season they will benefit from as many bad calls as they are the victim of.

A good manager is like a good referee. Managers need to keep their employees safe (from harassment, injury, and liability) and keep them on track to the goal of the project.

There is always a tension between process and flexibility. We have all worked on projects and in organizations that were either completely freewheeling or drowning in process, with too much of the latter typically resulting from too much of the former. A good manager knows how to balance the specific lines of authority and procedures on a given project and the needs of the project itself. Staff behavior that violates company rules should be noted, but need not be punished in the moment; a manager can let a project continue and wait for a lull to pull an employee aside to say that the violation was seen and noted, and in the future will be punished.

Such judgment is difficult to hone. Referees have to have the experience to know when to let something go, when to blow the whistle, and when to pull someone aside or send them off. Good refs have to be able to reasonably tell the difference between bad behavior that does not detract from the goal and that which does. Good managers, like good referees, are objective and able to remove their emotions or friendships from the situation. Former rec league referee Dave Tyahla is a good friend, is largely responsible for my meeting my wife, and also never hesitated to call a foul or give me a yellow card when refereeing games in which I was playing.

Like referees, managers will make mistakes. Sometimes those mistakes hurt an employee or project, sometimes they help. Over time, hopefully those mistakes cancel each other out.

*Refereeing gives you the best seat in the house ... but you're not a passive observer. You need to be objective, but also keep the game moving.*

Dave Tyahla, former rec league referee and experienced manager and lobbyist

Dave Tyahla told me that reffing made him a better player because he better understood the game from the position of the official; he saw the game more fully and learned to anticipate the action sometimes two or three steps ahead of the play. Not only could he see the game from the middle of the action, he saw the game with the laws rather than the result in mind. Seeing the game from the position of the official made him better at being the object of officiating.

Management is the same. Putting non-managers in charge of projects, assigning them the responsibility to keep a project on track rather than work on a part of the project, can make them better employees. With experience keeping an eye on all of the parts of a project and what it takes to keep those parts moving in the right direction an employee gets a better understanding of how his part fits in to the whole.

Non-managers need not wait until they are assigned leadership roles to take them on. Non-mangers can volunteer to lead ad hoc working groups or tiger teams, or join local nonprofit boards that rely on volunteer participation. In seeking leadership positions, non-managers can learn not just how to manage but also how to be better staff members.

A final lesson from refereeing comes from Mary Harvey, the goalkeeper on the 1991 women's US World Cup winning team. Harvey notes that when emotions are running high, people are shouting all sorts of things (sometimes in different languages) and referees have to sort through the noise to hear the legitimate concerns and determine what to do about them. Players, coaches, and fans scream at the ref a lot. That the ref never screams back does not mean that the ref is deaf, does not care, or that all claims of injustice are unfounded. The best referees will sort through the appeals to find the basis of the complaint and calmly decide what to do about it. Sometimes a referee will consult with an assistant on the sidelines, sometimes the ref will have conversations with players on the field, and in the end the ref will make a decision. Referees are especially adept at telling the signal from the noise.

Offices often sound like sporting events. Emotions can run high at work, especially when people are tired, working on tight deadlines, or when the stakes feel especially high. Under such conditions, people do not always calmly explain their positions in the hopes of having a robust dialogue about professional infractions and preferred outcomes. Instead, people often shout. They shout at their managers, at their peers, and at their staff. People shout at whoever happens to be in front of them in the moment they feel aggrieved.

The best managers are able to calmly hear through the noise to find what, if anything, merits acting on. Sometimes when staff or managers shout they are wrong. But there is usually something worth paying attention to through the ranting. By remaining calm and finding the nugget of legitimate complaint, the best managers and staff are able to keep focused on the goal at hand and adjust what they are doing as needed to keep moving toward that goal.

## Locker Room Notes for Managers

Keep your focus on the point of the work and keep everyone moving in that direction – sometimes that means letting infractions go or noting them after the fact.

Listen for legitimate complaints or concerns in the middle of others putting pressure on you, look for the signal in the middle of the noise.

Give junior staff opportunities to manage so they can see all that goes into a project or effort, not just their usual piece of it.

## Locker Room Notes for Staff

Talk to your managers about concerns without yelling. In those conversations draw attention to the impact of others' behavior on the goal, not on you or the specific rule being violated.

Find ways to manage projects or otherwise see the organization as a system and not just your part in that system.

## Endnotes

1.  Soccer has laws, not rules.
2.  A severe foul can result in a yellow card. If a player receives two yellow cards in a game he gets a red card and is sent off for the rest of the game. A player that has been sent off cannot be replaced; the team has to play short-handed for the rest of the game. A very severe foul can result in an immediate red card and sending off. Most red cards result in the player being banned from at least the next match, and often several matches, though the team doesn't have to play with ten players in those games.

# Chapter 16

# Advice for Managers

Most of this book is written for most people in an organization. But some lessons are more from coaches than players, the men and women on the sidelines screaming and pointing, kicking water bottles while their expensive suits get ruined in the rain.

> *The manager has to give you the blueprint and when you do go out you feel confident. And then good managers I think really they're the ones that once the players get some momentum that the players feel that they're responsible and have a bit of ownership over it and they set the tone, they set the discipline, set the respect, set the standard for each other, but I think it's about the manager first creating that environment.*
>
> Graeme La Saux, former professional and player on England's men's national team, "Pundits at the Lane"

The lessons in this chapter may not be immediately applicable to those who are not yet a manager (in other words, you can skip this section if you are not a manager and you are in a hurry). But if you do want to manage or better understand your manager, this chapter might be a good investment of time.

Former US men's national team player and NBC analyst Kyle Martino says a good coach is one who makes, "You feel prepared, you feel protected, you feel like you know what your job is individually, but also how you fit into the collective." In describing a good soccer manager, Martino's fellow commentator and former player Robbie Mustoe said, "Managers can have a style that can be very different ... I don't think [the style] is the key factor ... I want a plan, I want my manager to give us a set strategy of what we're trying to do on a match-day ... I want to know what my job is, I want to be accountable."

There are a few additional lessons for managers as well.

## Winning Isn't About You – But Losing Is

The post-game press conference is an international ritual. Right after a stunning victory or crushing defeat, the winner and loser are expected to praise their opponent and explain why their ability or inability to execute the game plan and their luck or lack of luck, led to the win or loss. These rituals rarely reveal much unless the coach or player on the podium says something especially stupid or especially funny (for example the player who thanked both his wife and girlfriend on television after an important win). An important part of the ritual is the coach taking responsibility for failure, and giving credit for success to the team.

Coaches may take the blame for a team's loss, even if that blame isn't deserved. But the coach should also give credit to the team when they win. A big part of the reason Bruce Arena is the most successful American coach of all time is that some of the best American players of all time were at their peak when he happened to take over the US Men's National Team. Arena put players like Claudio Reyna, Landon Donovan, and Christian Pulisic in a position to succeed – but Reyna, Donovan, and Pulisic were the ones on the field. Players want to play for managers who put the players first, who put the focus on those on the field not those on the sidelines.

Good managers do the same. While they own the mistakes of the team, good managers draw attention to team victories. The person attending executive meetings, tracking productivity, and talking the most during pitches is usually not the person making the sales calls, assembling the products, and otherwise writing the slides. Good managers know that by highlighting the work of doing the work, the work will better.

Coaches know that publicly defending their players – even if criticism is deserved and everyone knows it – keeps up morale and makes all the players more loyal and more likely to work hard. Occasionally publicly criticizing players can sometimes motivate them, but generally such criticism does nothing to effect the outcome of the game that just ended, and typically makes it that much harder to prepare for the next game.

> *'They're good, we're not – at the moment — and it's on me to fix it,'* [DC United head coach Ben] Olsen said.
> Steve Goff, 'They're good, we're not': DC United again comes up empty at home, Washington Post Soccer Insider"

A good coach also takes responsibility for the team's failures. The coach tells the press that he did not prepare the team well enough, that he put players in positions that they should not have been in, or that he had the wrong plan. Even if these things are not true – the best coach in the world still sits on the sideline, if a player misses an open goal or loses the guy he was supposed to be defending it is not the fault of the person watching the game from the bench – the coach owns the mistakes of the team. A player who makes the mistake that costs the game knows it was his or her fault, but by publicly owning the mistake the coach tells the player, "I've got your back" which makes the player work that much harder next time.

This, of course, is all in public. In the locker room or in the coach's office, the coach absolutely holds players accountable for their mistakes (as do the other players). And if the coach is any good he also owns his own mistakes to the players. Everyone on the team, players and coaches, hold each other accountable.

Good managers in organizations do the same. When you meet with your reports, either in a group or individually, you should hold each other accountable. You should call out their mistakes and take responsibility for your own mistakes. As a group you need to then learn from those mistakes and minimize the chance of them happening again. As a group, you and your staff are responsible to each other as you all are responsible to the organization and its mission.

When you meet with your fellow managers, part of your responsibility is to defend your staff. If they made mistakes, own them. Acknowledge the problem, say that you and your staff have discussed it and are making the appropriate adjustments, and that your staff will continue to succeed. If there is blame to be placed, you should assume it. Shuffling blame to your staff – even if it is obviously deserved – does nothing to correct the mistake, makes you look weak and ineffectual, and will ultimately get back to your staff which will undermine your efforts to excel. There is no upside to throwing your staff under the bus. Praise your staff for what they do well, take responsibility for their mistakes.

You should not throw your fellow managers under the bus either. As a group of managers you need to work together and for each other. You need to promote your boss's decisions to your team, and your direct reports should promote your decisions to their staff. Behind closed doors be frank, in public be supportive.

## Your Team Follows Your Emotional Lead

*It's an emotional game, and emotions always go both ways. When things go well, emotions skyrocket suddenly. If you lose a game, the emotions go in the other direction. As a coach, you have to live with that and keep your balance ...*
US men's national team head coach Jurgen Klinsmann after the US beat Guatemala 4-0, four days after losing to the same side 2-0, "US Men dominate Guatemala in World Cup qualifier"

Part of a soccer coach's job is keeping a team focused. After an unexpected win, emotions can run high and players can get over-confident going into the next game. After an unexpected loss, emotions can run high and not have enough confidence. A good coach knows that his players and team will reflect his demeanor. As such, a good coach will remain focused and level-headed from game to game. During games some coaches go nuts, while others are stoic no matter what. But over the course of a season or tournament such as the World Cup, coaches know to focus on the big picture. Their focus helps the players focus.

The same is true of organizations. Your staff looks to you for emotional and professional cues. If you are excited, they will be excited. If you are focused, they will be focused.

A young staffer at an organization at which I worked was playing a lead role on a big event for the first time. Not everything was going to plan – it never does – and the young staffer was pretty stressed about it. At one point he asked me to intervene to solve a problem. I was calm, the staffer calmed down, and everything went fine. After the event the staffer thanked me for just being relaxed and helping him see that little problems are just that – little. As long as the event was on track, and as long as the larger purpose the event was serving was on track, then everything was fine.

## The Best Players aren't always the Best Managers

The sports world is littered with great players who were terrible coaches and managers. In soccer there may be no better example than Argentina's Diego Maradona.

Maradona is one of the best soccer players of all time, with only Pele, Johan Cruyff, and Lionel Messi even in the same conversation. His goals against England in the 1986 World Cup – one scored illegally with his hand (or as he put it, "the hand of god") and one a dizzying display of footwork that beat nearly the entire English – are among the most famous in the history of soccer. Yet he coached Argentina to the worst losses in the team's history and was fired after getting routed 4-0 by Germany in the quarterfinals of the World Cup.

*"Nobody ever told me where to play. So I shouldn't have to tell [Lionel] Messi where to play, either," Maradona said.*
ESPN.com "Argentina Won't Retain Maradona"

On the other hand, some exceedingly mediocre players – and some players who never even reached that height – have gone on to successful coaching careers. José Mourinho, who is among the best coaches of the past several decades, peaked as a semi-professional player in Portugal. Arsene Wenger, who is among the most respected coaches in the world and who helped change professional soccer in England, similarly rose no further than semi-professional play spending most of his playing career in either assistant coaching roles or with student and amateur teams. The best coaches America has produced, Bruce Arena and Bob Bradley, have a combined one year of semi-professional soccer (Arena spent a year as backup goalkeeper for the Takoma Tides – he also played professional lacrosse for a year) and a total of 45 minutes with the National Team (Arena was a second half substitute in goal in a 2-0 loss to Israel). Bradley's playing career ended when he graduated from Princeton University. Both have gone on to lead the US Men's National Team into the elimination rounds of the World Cup and Major League Soccer teams to championships. Bradley also has coached the men's national team in Egypt and coached professionally in Norway and France, and was the first American in charge of a team in England's Premier League (a forgettable 11 games at Swansea, but the first American manager in the Premiership none the less).

Some great players have lead great teams. Pep Guardiola has won as a player and a manager and Johan Cruyff was a visionary coach and player who helped create the modern game. But many coaches were pretty good players who worked hard on the field and work hard on the sidelines.

A challenge a gifted player has in making the transition to coaching is that they were gifted players. It didn't make sense to Maradona to have to tell players where to play – they should just know because he just knew. But "do it better" or "do it like I do it" is useless advice. And if a player could play like Maradona he would. Players who were only pretty good, or not good at all, often had to put more thought into their games in order to succeed. They had to figure out what the component parts of "better" are –where to look, where to move, and when to run. They had to work to solve the complex problems of a simple game. As such, they can be both more patient and more specific when coaching others. They know the frustration of trying to get something right, and know what the elements of "right" look like. Because they had to work to be good players, they can help others work to be good players as well.

Similarly, the best player may not make the best captain. In soccer a team captain sets the team's tone, resolves disputes, and keeps his colleagues working together in the system. The captain often resolves disputes with the referee. The captain is the most respected player on a team, but not necessarily the best player.

*Every team has somebody that others aspire to be or who they respect because they conduct themselves in the right way. They may not be the best player, but they are someone to look up to.*
Frank Hilldrup, former Virginia Tech player, Chief Technical Advisor International Aviation, National Transportation Safety Board

As a manager it can be tempting to promote your most talented specialists – to put outstanding analysts in charge of teams of analysts, and exceptional communications staff in charge of public affairs. Sometimes that is the right decision, but often it is not. The skills it takes to understand the complex interactions of multiple streams of data are not necessarily the ones needed to get other data scientists to drive the corporate mission. Anyone who has spent any time anywhere near a law firm knows that good attorneys are often terrible managers of other attorneys (or of paralegals, accounting, support staff, or anyone else for that matter). Being good at something and helping others get better at something are different skills.

In an organization, as on the soccer field, leaders emerge from the process. Those leaders may not be the most talented staff or the most gifted sales people or programmers; the leaders are those who set a good example for their colleagues and who make everyone around them better.

## Clear and Consistent Feedback

Soccer players want to know what is expected of them, what they have to do to start a game on the field rather than on the bench, and if they are on the bench what they have to do to get on the field. A former professional player told me that the best coaches he had were the ones who gave clear and consistent feedback. He told you when you did something wrong and how to fix it. When you did something right he praised you and told you how to get better next time. You might not agree with the coach's decision to start you or not play you at all, but you were never surprised.

The same is true in organizations. More and more companies are turning away from the annual review and moving more toward ongoing coaching. The old annual or bi-annual review is being replaced with constant interaction. A soccer coach would not set a line-up at the beginning of a season and leave it intact and unchanged for the year. Neither should managers in organizations.

*... employees need instant performance management — that is, ongoing performance development — to know when they're moving in the right direction or how to make a positive change. As GE's*

*head of human resources Susan Peters recently put it, 'The world isn't really on an annual cycle any more for anything.'*
Kris Duggin, "Why the Annual Performance Review is Going Extinct"

The best managers let their reports know what is working and why, what is not working and why, and how to get better. Clear and consistent feedback – "keep your memos to one page with bullets" is good, "write better" is bad – helps staff improve in the moment they need it. "That thing I think I recall you doing several months ago should have been done differently" is flat awful.

## Sell Yourself

*Perception may not be everything, but it's a heck of a lot. It's not just about keeping your job, either. If you can't 'sell' internally, players lose faith. And then poor performances become a self-fulfilling prophecy.*
Gabriele Marcotti, "Why managers always need to be selling to get – and keep – their jobs"

A common refrain from sports commentators is the players have "bought into the system" the coach established (or have failed to buy in). A coach has to persuade the players – all of whom are very good at what they do and in many cases are better players than the coach ever was – that the system is the right one for the team to succeed. The coach also has to sell the team's owners on the approach since they are the ones paying the bills. Players, fans, and owners read the papers and social media and they all watch TV. If the media is behind a coach it is easier to keep the fans, owners, and players on board so selling the approach to the media is important as well. If the fans do not buy the approach games can get awfully unpleasant for everyone, they increase pressure on owners, and the media covers discontent which puts more pressure on the coach and players.

On rec league teams the stakes are not as high, and the systems not as formal. Unlike in the pros, there is virtually no enforcement mechanism on rec league teams – players who don't buy in don't get benched, cut, or traded. The captain or organizer of a rec league team has an even tougher job of selling a system because there are no penalties for misbehaving. But it is no less important for players to buy into a system for a rec league team to succeed.

A friend of mine named Kizito has organized a team in a local coed rec league for a number of years. At the start the team was made up of his friends and a few friends of theirs, and there wasn't much of an approach beyond players showing up and sorting it out. The team had a fair amount of fun but didn't win a lot of games. Kizito is pretty competitive and wanted to both have fun and win so he looked at his players, and developed a system. As players left the team because they moved or found better things to do on Saturday afternoons he replaced them with others who were better skilled and wanted to play his system. The team started to win. Kizito kept selling his system as he talked to new players he was thinking about inviting to the team and to the current players in pre-game huddles, during half-time talks, and after the game. He never stops selling his system, the players buy the sales pitch, and the team is winning.

Managers in organizations have the same challenges. Managers need to persuade their reports that the system for the unit is a good one, and the staff need to understand, be able to execute, and buy-into the manager's system. The staff have to believe that the approach taken by the manager is a good one, and be willing to put their best into making the system succeed. No system is self-evidently brilliant, and people are used to working in lots of systems so the successful manager needs to sell the system while helping ensure the system itself works.

*(Arsenal coach Arsene Wenger) likened managing a club to running a corporation. The difference was that a CEO will get judged by shareholders – at worst – every quarter. A manager gets it after every game.*
Gabriele Marcotti, "Why managers always need to be selling to get – and keep – their jobs"

In addition to selling the system to his or her subordinates, the manager needs to sell the system to his or her superiors as well. If the next person up the org chart doesn't believe the approach taken by the manager is the right one, the manager will not last. At the most senior level, if shareholders or the board do not believe in the system, the CEO is out.

*You have to get buy-in. People have to feel that they are part of a solution ... People have to have a sense of mission, all other components are less important. In organizations, if people feel that they are part of a mission, they will fight to the end and exceed expectations. They are also more likely to succeed.*
Antonio Soave, Former Kansas Secretary of Commerce, Chairman and CEO of Capistrano Global Advisory Services, former head coach at Ave Maria University in Florida and Franciscan University of Steubenville in Ohio, and former semi-professional player

As a manager you need a clear vision of where you want to go and how you want to get there, and you have to communicate that vision to those who work for you and to those for whom you work.

A lot of management is like pro soccer. Even if you are not the Arsene Wenger of your industry, leading one of the world's most profitable and high profile brands, you have to persuade those with a financial stake in your success that your approach is the right one. Like Wenger, you have to get your staff to buy into your approach – and like Wenger you can fire those who do not step up.

But a lot of management is more like rec league soccer than the pros. Staff at all levels are often put in informal management settings – running "tiger teams" or coordinating coalition meetings or working groups. A relatively junior staff member may be asked to play a convening or informal management role as a "first among equals" on a project. And as with all management that staff member will need a system and will need to get those on the project and those to whom he reports to buy into that system. Failure in these informal roles can stall a career because they may demonstrate managerial weakness – and success in these roles can accelerate a career because it shows an ability to organize and lead.

# Chapter 17

# Advice for Staff

Most of this book is directed at everyone in an organization, those who manage and those who are managed alike. But some advice is more suited for those do not manage much, if at all. This chapter is for those folks, the new players on a team who need to work their way into the lineup.

*The graveyards are full of indispensable men.*
Often attributed to Charles De Gaulle

## Respect is Earned

*French people are very introverted, so it took me a little longer to get into the group. I had to earn respect and it took almost four months – until I scored my first goal – for my teammates to start opening up. All of a sudden, guys who I didn't think spoke any English started speaking a little bit of English to me.*
US player Alejandro Bedoya on making the transition to the French team FC Nantes, The Players Tribune

Players who show up on the field acting as if they are the Next Best Thing without earning it quickly find themselves isolated on the field. Players don't pass them the ball and don't bail them out when they are in trouble. The result is that the player quickly finds himself on the bench, then cut from the team entirely. Everyone on every team has to earn respect every play.

World Cup winning goalkeeper Mary Harvey notes that no one applauds the first time you walk into a locker room. You have to earn the respect of your teammates. Ben Olsen, whose name appears all over this book, is an example of a player who worked hard every day as a player to earn the respect of his teammates and the fans. He works equally hard as a coach. At his best, Ben was among the best: he was the nation's high school and college player of the year, Major League Soccer rookie of the year, MVP of the MLS championship game, MLS all-star, and he played in both the Olympics and World Cup. He was a relentless and tenacious player, something that served him well as he aged and injuries took their toll. Ben worked hard every minute of every game, throwing his body and considerable skills at every play. He has done the same as a coach. He works hard at working hard. As a result, Washington DC adores him; the iconic Ben's Chili Bowl, a chili-dog restaurant that served lunch to both police and protesters during the 1968 riots and the last place President Barack Obama had lunch before taking the oath of office changed its name to Ben Olsen's Chili Bowl for a day.

The same is true at work. Your co-workers at your new job were at the organization before you were, and many will be there when you leave. Those who get hired after you likely have no idea who you are.

You may have gotten a job that one or more of your new co-workers applied for and did not get. You may have been chosen above some of their friends. In nearly any position at any organization, you have taken someone else's job. You cannot get respect by expecting it, you have to earn it.

You earn respect first and foremost by being respectful. This means not being dismissive of colleagues or ideas, listening more than talking, preparing for meetings and events, doing the boring work well and without complaint, and not emailing or texting during meetings or conversations. Prove that you are someone who has the best interest of the organization at heart, and that you are someone willing to work hard to help the unit achieve the organization's goals.

## Seize Your Moments

In 2004 the US Men's national soccer team was locked in tough labor negotiations with the US Soccer Federation. The talks were so tough that the players threatened to go on strike right before a round of important World Cup qualifying games. To ensure that the US would field a team, should the strike happen, the Federation cut a deal with a lower-division professional league in the US to bring in their top players. The strike never happened but one of those lower-division players, Clyde Simms, caught the eye of the US coach and Simms landed a contract with DC United. A year later, Simms earned his first call-up to the full national team. He went on to a successful career with DC and the New England Revolution before kidney disease prematurely ended his career. Simms' chance came as a result of elements well out of his control, and when that chance came he seized it.

In 1993 I helped make then-US Representative Sam Coppersmith (D-Ariz.) the first member of Congress with a presence on the internet. It was a lowly gopher-server.[1] Senator Kennedy became the second member of Congress online when he launched his web page.[2] In 1994 Coppersmith ran for the Senate and lost, and I wound up a reporter in Phoenix. In researching a story on a federal program I called Chris Casey, Senator Kennedy's internet guy. Chris said he didn't know anything about the program, and that the next day was his last with the Senator, and did I know anyone who wanted to take his place? I suggested a friend who I thought was going to the Peace Corps but might be interested. "No, Peter, do you want my job?" A week later I flew out to interview and a few weeks later was living in Washington, maintaining Senator Kennedy's computers and network, and running his webpage.

The problem of course is that I had no idea how to do any of those things. I had never built or managed a computer network and had never written a webpage (in my defense, in 1995 a lot of people hadn't written webpages). I was comfortable with computers and had done rudimentary programming in high school, and had persuaded the Maricopa County Democratic Party to get email (seems astonishing now that anyone had to be talked into email; 1992 was a long time ago in internet time). But a passing knowledge of Fortan and Basic hardly qualified me to write HTML or run a network. And yet there I was in the Russell Senate Office Building doing just that. In my year with the Senator I only crashed the network once, learned how to write HTML (a skill I still use from time to time), and landed the Senator as the first federal elected official to do an online chat on America Online back when that sort of thing was a big deal.

If you are given the chance to step up, step up. Know that you are being given the chance because someone believes you can do it, so even if you do not have confidence in yourself have confidence in them.

## Learn Constantly

*The legendary coach José Mourinho led a team in Portugal called Porto to the league championship, the Portuguese Cup[3] and what was then the UEFA Cup in which the top professional teams across Europe compete (the competition is now known as the Champions League). He was concerned that the success would lead the team to be complacent in the following season, so to keep them thinking and growing as players he changed the formation. Rather than let the players rest on their well-earned laurels, Mourihno forced his players to learn a new system and new approach, which kept the players thinking and focused.*
Luís Lourenço, José Mourinho Special Leadership: Creating and Managing Successful Teams

Paying attention to learning keeps players at all levels sharp and improving. The mental engagement ensures in-game focus. As players age or suffer injuries that slow them down or limit their mobility, attention to learning ensures they can continue to play and contribute. If you are a player who relies on speed and fitness for success, you need to learn positioning as you get older and slow down. If you keep playing and hips and knees do not quite do what they used to do, you need to find ways to use your body differently to win and protect the ball. Learning on the field keeps you paying attention and succeeding in the moment while simultaneously setting you up for the next challenges and the next moment.

*From youth soccer on up, the game is the teacher.*
Len Oliver, writer and consultant, National Soccer Hall of Fame, former professional player and member of the US Olympic Team

Ben Olsen was forced to learn to play smarter soccer after a series of ankle injuries took away some of his quickness. To keep playing at a top level, Ben had to learn better positioning and how to be a smarter player to make up for what he lost in speed and mobility. This commitment to learning not only kept his playing career going – it also makes him a better coach because he was forced to think about the game as a player. He sees how players and the game can change because he had to change to keep in the game.

The same is true at work. The moment you stop learning is the moment you stop thinking, and that is the moment you stall. The best staff members with whom I have worked are those who are good at what they do, and who are always looking to add a new skill to their portfolio or find ways to keep improving the skills they've got. The above quoted Len Oliver points out that just as a player learns from other players on the field, good staff learn from their colleagues at work. Good staff pay attention to what their colleagues do well, and what they do less well, and learn from what they see.

This book is in part the result of that urge to keep learning. Early in my career I was given supervisory responsibility – I was asked to manage – without any training or support. I did reasonably well because I knew how to do the work which I was managing others to do, and my teams were small. And to be honest, in politics the bar for what counts as good management is pretty low. As I was given more responsibility it became increasingly clear that simply doing more of the same when it came to management was not going to cut it, so I began to seek input from others. When I became the first VP for External Relations at the US Institute of Peace I assembled an informal management advisory kitchen cabinet, and began to devour management books and articles. This commitment to learning made me better at managing and made my non-management work better. An additional benefit is that my staff saw that I took management seriously and they worked harder with me. I also rewarded members of my staff who made concerted efforts to improve existing skills or learn new ones. At USIP my team had access to funds for professional development and with those funds members of my staff received management coaching, earned a master's degree, took courses in digital video editing, and more. My concern was less that the skill was immediately applicable to the work, than it was in my staff engaging in the process of learning (and to Kyle Martino's point about why Bruce Arena was such a good coach, it demonstrated that I was invested in the careers of my staff).

As you think about your work and your career, keep thinking. If your employer provides funds for professional development, use them. You will pick up new skills and demonstrate to your boss that you want to learn new skills, which is something good bosses reward. If you do not have access to professional development funds (or even if you do), figure out what you can learn from your colleagues. Look around at who is valued at your office or what skills always seem to be in demand, then find the person at your office who is the best at it, and ask if you can help in exchange for learning. Again, you'll get valuable skills and demonstrate that you are a good colleague, both of which good bosses reward.

## Keep Playing

Soccer players make tons of mistakes. You get kicked and hit by the ball in uncomfortable places, yelled at by the coach, teammates and fans. You play in the rain, snow and cold. There are times when it feels like nothing is going right, you will never be dry and warm, and everything hurts. But you keep playing – you have to. Professional soccer teams are typically allowed to make only three substitutions over 90 minutes of playing, and once taken out of a game a player isn't allowed to go back in. If you're having a bad day you've got to put your head down and keep playing.

An American player named Brian McBride became my lovely young wife's favorite player the day after Christmas in 2005. McBride was playing for an unheralded team in London called Fulham FC. They were playing their local rivals, the high-flying Chelsea at Chelsea's Stamford Bridge stadium on Boxing Day, December 26th. Shortly after Chelsea scored their first goal McBride came out the worse in a collision and he left the field with a huge cut on his head. McBride was off the field for nearly 10 minutes getting stitches – bear in mind that in soccer had Fulham replaced McBride with another player, McBride couldn't have come back on. McBride finally re-entered the game with a massive bandage covering his stiches and scored five minutes later. The team needed him to deal with the pain and blood, and play. So he played. US women's national team goalkeeper Mary Harvey gave up a soft goal right before the halftime of the World Cup final in 1991 – she came back onto the field after the half and helped her team win the first Women's World Cup. The team needed her to put the mistake behind her and play. So she played.

It is easier in rec league soccer. Most leagues allow unlimited substitutions, and you can go back in a game as often as you would like. But your teammates still rely on you to put in a solid shift so they can rest. Your teammates count on you to work as hard as you can so the team can succeed. In pickup it isn't an issue – if you're done, you're done. There are usually a couple of people waiting to take your place. But if you want to get better you've got to keep going. You've got other people counting on you, all of whom are also cold and wet, kicked and hurt.

> *When I was playing with high quality teams, I was shocked to find that I didn't always enjoy the training, preparation and games. The 24/7 focus is difficult and it was probably less fun than fun sometimes. The pressure and expectation is a constant and the fitness can literally be painful. Same with work ... there is a lot of stuff at work that just isn't fun and requires pain and discomfort; that is also true of most great wins or engaging complex challenges at work or in your community.*
>
> Neil Richardson, Founder Emergent Action, co-author of *Preparing for a World that Doesn't Exist – Yet*, former professional soccer player Richmond Kickers

The same things happen at work. Work isn't always fun (that's why they call it work). Computers crash and networks go down. Heat goes out in buildings and subway systems sometimes close. Your boss isn't always (or ever) nice to you, and your colleagues may not be much better. Your clients may take you for granted and it may seem like you will never close another deal. In the face of all of these challenges, these bits of sand in the shoe that can quickly go from irritating to excruciating, you have to keep going. You have to make the next pitch call. You have to present bad news to the boss who hates getting bad news. You have to get to work by bus or bike. You may need to wear a coat at your desk. Whatever the challenge, you need to keep working.

Similarly, if you make a mistake, keep going. This is different than blowing an event that you can debrief about later (see the chapter called Failure and Fame are Fleeting for more on that) – this is about making a mistake in the middle of an event (or meeting, presentation, or whatever) and keeping going. If you forget to order forks for the morning fruit and muffin spread, go get forks. If the projector stops working during your slide presentation keep going and talk folks through the visuals. If you say something stupid in a meeting, don't worry about it and keep on participating. If you make a mistake, keep going.

Plugging away through adversity will do the same things for you that it does for players. First, it makes you more likely to succeed. If you make a mistake and you quit trying (or worse yet quit altogether) you will have failed. Second, by keeping going through adversity you are not only more likely to succeed, but you also demonstrate to those around you that you do not give up on them and your shared mission. By giving up on a play, a player lets down himself and everyone else on the team; by continuing to play, the player demonstrates grit and leadership that can serve as an example for others.

## Endnotes

1. People could come and get text files from a central server. It was called a "gopher" because the technology was developed at the University of Minnesota where the school mascot is a gopher, sadly not because users could "go-fer" information. Our office was approached by Arizona State University professor Steve Corman about trying the service – the idea was Professor Corman's, we just said yes.

2. Credit here goes to Eric Loeb, then at the Massachusetts Institute of Technology and the Senator's system administrator at the time Chris Casey.

3.  Most countries have a tournament in which every team in the country can play, from the lowest amateur side to the top professional team. Like the NCAA basketball tournament, it's single elimination, and as with the NCAA basketball tournament there are always upsets and Cinderella stories. Teams rarely win both their league and the tournament in the same year.

# Chapter 18

# Added Time

From World Cup winners to rec league and pickup players a few themes echoed across my interviews.

First, soccer is global watercooler talk. No matter who you talk to, you can use a soccer metaphor to explain an idea. No matter where you go, you can start a conversation by talking about the game.

Second, soccer forces you to think globally. Because the game is international, and teams inevitably have people from different countries and backgrounds, you are forced to see the world from different perspectives. On the field no one really cares if you are an Ambassador or a house painter – you can hit a pass or you can't, you're a good teammate or you're not. One of the things I love about playing in Washington DC is that soccer is the only place I go where the conversation doesn't start with "who do you work for?" I had no idea that one of the people I interviewed for this book, Ambassador Arturo Sarukhan, was anything more than a goalkeeper on my over-45 rec league team until I saw him play in a charity match. When I met him on the field sevearal years ago his title didn't matter – what mattered was that he was a good teammate.

Finally, and most importantly, if you're at all smart you learn from the game. Soccer teaches you to solve problems in the moment. It forces you to collaborate. The game teaches you not to let mistakes prevent you from trying again – and it forces you to be humble when you succeed. Soccer teaches you to see beyond your own two feet.

There are far more lessons for managers and organizations – and for parenting, politics, and just about anything else that involves more than one person at a time. There are also things that happen in soccer, or around soccer, that may offer lessons that do not quite fit in a book about how successful organizations behave. Soccer, like society, is dealing with complex issues like corruption, racism, homophobia, and violence.

I have set up www.SoccerThinking.com to keep learning from the game. The site includes guest posts, interviews, and more that bring lessons from soccer to the rest of the world (and sometimes lessons from the rest of the world to soccer). If you like what you read here and are thinking "yah but what about ..." check out the website. If your thought isn't there, let me know and maybe we can add it, after all what is soccer if not an ongoing conversation?

See you around the pitch.

# List of Interviews

A lot of people were very generous with their time and input. Everyone I talked to provided interesting insight, though not all of them are directly quoted in this book.

Ken Alexander
Manager at a large consulting firm and former professional player

Amr Aly
Partner, Mayer Brown, former US Men's Olympic and National teams, college player of the year, and former professional player

Ashley Starks Amin
Social entrepreneur/fellow, former management consultant, former player The George Washington University

Kizito Byenkya
Program Specialist Open Society Foundations, rec league team manager and player

Ander Caballero
Delegate of the Basque Country to the United States, former COO Progenika, former amateur soccer player

Alan Dietrich
Chief Operating Officer, Sporting KC (Major League Soccer)

Roger Frank
Managing Director and Founder Innovare Advisors, Chairman of the Board of Directors, FarmDrive, former semi-professional player

Ari Gejdenson
Founder and CEO, Mindful Restaurants, former professional player in Bolivia, Chile, and Italy

Mary Harvey
Principal, Ripple Effect Consulting, World Cup winner, Olympic gold medalist, former member US Soccer board of directors, former Director of Development at FIFA (world governing body of soccer, at the time the highest ranking woman at FIFA), Hall of Fame member for: US Olympic Committee, Cal Athletics, American Youth Soccer Organization, Winner Werner Fricker Award from US Soccer (highest honor for soccer in the United States), US Soccer Medal of Honor (1991 Team)

Jerry Hauser
CEO, The Management Center, lifelong mediocre pickup player

Frank Hilldrup, Chief Technical Advisor, International Aviation, National Transportation and Safety Board, former Virginia Tech player

Sean Hinkle
Chief Program Officer at DC SCORES, founder of Ragball International, captained University of Virginia men's soccer team

Chris Jones
Coach, Entrepreneur & Host of The Tech LowDown podcast, member of the Georgetown University Hall of Fame, former captain of Hollywood United FC amateur soccer team

Danny Karbassiyoon
Co-Founder and Product Lead, Sports Without Limits (SWOL) and Fury90, author of *The Arsenal Yankee*, first American to score

at Arsenal

Lori Lindsey
Former US Women's National Team and professional player, soccer trainer, human rights advocate

Alex Aranzábal Mínguez
Partner AYA – Aguirre y Aranzabal and former President of SD Eibar 2009-2016 in La Liga

Daniel Neal
CEO & Founder, Kajeet Inc, former player University of Rochester

Len Oliver
Writer, consultant. Inducted into seven Soccer Halls of Fame, including the National Soccer Hall of Fame and the Virginia-DC Soccer Hall of Fame, former professional player and member of the US Olympic Team

Ben Olsen
Head coach, DC United. Parade Magazine high school player of the year, Soccer America College Player of the Year, Major League Soccer Rookie of the Year, Major League Soccer Cup Most Valuable Player, US Soccer Young Male Athlete of the Year, member US Olympic Team, member US Men's National Team including a World Cup appearance, Major League Soccer Coach of the Year.

Kevin Payne
CEO US Club Soccer, one of the founders of Major League Soccer, Founder and former President and CEO of DC United and former President and General Manager of Toronto FC, and longtime US Soccer Board member.

Raj Purohit
Real estate professional, coach, human rights lecturer and lifelong Spurs fan

Neil Richardson
Founder Emergent Action, co-author of Preparing for a World that Doesn't Exist – Yet, former professional soccer player Richmond Kickers

Jonas Rolett
Special Advisor to the Chairman Open Society Foundations, left it all on the field

Sonia Ruiz-Bolanos
Councilmember Gerson Lehrman Group, former Managing Director of Johns Hopkins Medicine International, played intermural at the University of Maryland and in rec leagues around the Washington, DC metro area

Ambassador Arturo Sarukhan
Mexican Ambassador to the United States 2007-2013, goalkeeper, What 4 over-45 team in Montgomery County, Maryland

Antonion Soave
Former Kansas Secretary of Commerce, Chairman and CEO of Capistrano Global Advisory Services (CGA), former head coach at Ave Maria University in Florida and Franciscan University of Steubenville in Ohio, and former semi-professional player

Brian Straus
Sports Illustrated writer, former youth coach and player

Dave Tyahla
Long-time amateur and semi-pro level referee and experienced

policy analyst, manager and lobbyist

Tanya Vogel
Senior Associate Athletics Director, The George Washington University, former player and head coach at GW, member of the GW Athletics Hall of Fame

Sarah Warren, Ed.L.D.
Education and non-profit leader, former player and captain, Haverford College Women's Soccer

Michael Williamson
Chief Strategy Officer, F.C. Internazionale Milano (Inter Milan)

Antonio Zea
Senior Director, Global Soccer Footwear, Under Armour, lifelong Real Madrid fan

# References

*The Away End* (2016) 'Skill is decision making, not scissors', 1 March [Online] http://www.theawayendfooty.com/the-home-front/2016/3/1/skill-is-decision-making-not-scissors (Accessed 29 June 29, 2017).

*BBC.com* (2017) 'Birmingham City: Harry Redknapp has galvanised Blues, says skipper Morrison', 8 May [Online] Available at http://www.bbc.com/sport/football/39846345 (Accessed 29 June 2017).

Bedoya, Alejandro (2016) 'U.S. player Alejandro Bedoya on making the transition to the French team FC Nantes, "Why I Love Playing Abroad"', *The Players Tribune* 22 April [Online] http://www.theplayerstribune.com/alejandro-bedoya-soccer-usmnt-fc-nantes-france/ (Accessed 29 June 2017).

Bell, Jack (2013) 'Phil Woosman, Pioneer of North American Soccer Dies at 80', *The New York Times*, 21 July [Online] Available at http://www.nytimes.com/2013/07/22/sports/soccer/phil-woosnam-pioneer-of-north-american-soccer-dies-at-80.html (Accessed 29 June 2017).

Blank, Dan (2012) *Soccer IQ: Things That Smart Players Do* Charleston, SC: Self-published

Bokeno, R. Michael (2009) 'An Alternative Sports Metaphor for Understanding Teamwork as Complex: Soccer' *E:CO*, vol. 11 no. 2 pp. 79-86.

Carlisle, Jeff (2015) 'How Getting Cut Helped Carli Lloyd Refocus And Find Her Spot On The USWNT', *ESPNW. Com* 3 June [Online] http://www.espn.com/espnw/news-commentary/2015worldcup/article/13006977/how-getting-cut-helped-carli-lloyd-refocus-find-spot-us-women-national-team (Accessed 7 June 2017).

Cassman, Joel F. and David Lai (2003) 'Football vs Soccer: American Warfare in an Era of Unconventional Threats'

*Armed Forces Journal*, November pp. 49-54.

Cohn, Patrick (2016) 'How do you (or your soccer players) respond to mistakes?', *Soccer Psychology Tips* 14 January [Online] http://www.soccerpsychologytips.com/2014/confident-after-mistakes-soccer (Accessed 29 June 2017).

Crotty, James Marshall (2015) 'Like a Good Referee, the Next U.S. President Should Be Measured, Courageous, and Decidedly Not the Story' *Huff Post* 7 June [Online] http://www.huffingtonpost.com/james-marshall-crotty/like-a-good-referee-our-n_b_7739412.html (Accessed 9 June 2017).

Crowe, Jonathan (2014) 'Agile Lessons from the Most Innovative Team in World Cup History', *OpenView Labs*, 5 July [Online] http://labs.openviewpartners.com/total-football-agile-team-management/#.WTrgeWjyvIU (Accessed 29 June 2017).

Cruyff, Johan (2016) quoted in Steve Goff 'A tribute to Johan Cruyff, the Dutch soccer maestro' *Washington Post Soccer Insider* 24 March [Online] Available at https://www.washingtonpost.com/news/soccer-insider/wp/2016/03/24/a-tribute-to-johan-cruyff-the-dutch-soccer-maestro (Accessed 29 June 2017).

Duggin, Kris (2015) 'Why the Annual Performance Review is Going Extinct', *FastCompany online* 20 October [Online] Available at https://www.fastcompany.com/3052135/why-the-annual-performance-review-is-going-extinct (Accessed 29 June 2017).

*The Economist* (2015) 'Learning from Failure: What stops people from turning mistakes into success?' 10 October [Online] Available at http://www.economist.com/news/business-books-quarterly/21672015-what-stops-people-turning-mistakes-success-learning-failure (Accessed 29 June, 2017).

Elberse, Anita (2013) 'Ferguson's Formula' *Harvard Business Review online* October [Online] Available at https://hbr.org/2013/10/fergusons-formula (Accessed 29 May2017).

*ESPN.com news service* (2010) 'Argentina Won't Retain Maradona' 27 July [Online] Available at http://www.espn.com/sports/soccer/news/_/id/5414683/diego-maradona-head-coach-argentina-national-team (Accessed 29 June 2017).

Evans, Lisa (2016) 'How to Become the Most Well-Liked Person in the Office', *Fast Company online*, 5 February [Online] Available at https://www.fastcompany.com/3056333/work-smart/how-to-become-the-most-well-liked-person-in-the-office (Accessed 29 June 2017).

Fernando, Vincent (2009) 'When a CEO Becomes Famous, Fire Him' *Business Insider* 16 November [Online] Available at http://www.businessinsider.com/when-a-ceo-becomes-famous-fire-him-2009-11 (Accessed 29 June 2017).

Goff, Steven (2016) 'Wednesday Kick Around', *Washington Post Soccer Insider* 27 January [Online] Available at https://www.washingtonpost.com/news/soccer-insider/wp/2016/01/27/wednesday-kickaround-d-c-united-washington-spirit-americans-abroad/?postshare=2271453903803020&tid=ss_tw (Accessed 29 June 2017).

... (2016) 'U.S. Men dominate Guatemala in World Cup qualifier' *Washington Post Soccer Insider* 29 March [Online] Available at https://www.washingtonpost.com/sports/dcunited/us-men-dominate-guatemala-in-world-cup-qualifier/2016/03/29/5c05a186-f5e9-11e5-9804-537defcc3cf6_story.html?tid=a_inl (Accessed 29 May 2017).

... (2017) 'U.S. men seek to keep momentum going in World Cup qualifier vs. Panama', *Washington Post Soccer Insider* 27 March [Online] Available at https://www.washingtonpost.com/news/soccer-insider/wp/2017/03/27/u-s-men-seek-to-keep-momentum-going-in-world-cup-qualifier-vs-panama/?utm_term=.c38174079d22 (Accessed 29 June 2017).

... (2017) 'They're good, we're not': D.C. United again comes up empty at home, *Washington Post Soccer Insider*, 20 May [Online] Available at https://www.washingtonpost.com/

news/soccer-insider/wp/2017/05/20/theyre-good-were-not-d-c-uniteds-ben-olsen-takes-blame-after-loss-to-chicago/?utm_term=.4f15de22fe3c (Accessed 29 June 2017).

… (2017) 'After rough Premier League season, Brad Guzan aims for smooth transition at Copa America', *Washington Post Soccer Insider* 1 June [Online] Available at https://www.washingtonpost.com/news/soccer-insider/wp/2016/06/01/after-rough-premier-league-season-brad-guzan-aims-for-smooth-transition-at-copa-america/ (Accessed 29 June 2017).

Hein, Rich (2013) '16 Traits of Great It Leaders', *CIO.com* 23 October [Online] Available at http://www.cio.com/article/2381555/careers-staffing/16-traits-of-great-it-leaders.html (Accessed 29 June 2017).

*High Fidelity* (2000) Directed by Stephen Frears [Film] Los Angeles, Touchstone Pictures.

Hoffman, Reid (2014) 'The Alliance visual summary', Slideshare [Online] Available at https://www.slideshare.net/reidhoffman/the-alliance-a-visual-summary (Accessed 29 June 2017).

Hoffman, Reid, Ben Casnocha and Chris Yeh (2014) 'Your Company Is Not a Family' *Harvard Business Review online* 17 June [Online] Available at https://hbr.org/2014/06/your-company-is-not-a-family (Accessed 29 June 2017).

Jabr, Ferris (2013) 'Your Brain Needs More Downtime Than You Think', *Salon* 16 October [Online] Available at http://www.salon.com/2013/10/16/your_brain_needs_more_downtime_than_it_thinks_partner (Accessed 7 June 2017).

Jenewein, Wolfgang, Thomas Kochanek, Marcus Heidbrink and Christian Schimmelpfennig (2014) 'Learning Collaboration from Tiki-Taka Soccer', *Harvard Business Review* July [Online] Available at https://hbr.org/2014/07/learning-collaboration-from-tika-taka-soccer (Accessed 29 May 2017).

La Saux, Graeme (2017) *NBC Premiere League Download: Pundits at the Lane* [Online] Available at http://www.nbcsports.com/video/premier-league-download-pundits-lane (Accessed 29 June 2017).

Levy, Paul F. (2012) *Goal Play! Leadership Lessons from the Soccer Field*, Self-published.

Lourenço, Luis (2010 – English translation 2014) *José Mourinho: Special Leadership – Creating and Managing Successful Teams*, Estoril, Portugal: Prime Books.

Marcotti, Gabriele (2015) 'Why managers always need to be selling to get – and keep – their jobs', *ESPNFC.com* 28 October [Online] Available at http://www.espnfc.com/blog/marcottis-musings/62/post/2686327/gab-marcotti-on-managers-ability-to-sell-themselves (Accessed 29 May 2017).

Martino, Kyle (2017) *NBC Premiere League Download: Pundits at the Lane* [Online] Available at http://nbcsports.com/video/premier-league-download-pundits-lane (Accessed 29 May 2017).

Mertesaker, Per (2016) 'Arsenal FC captain Per Mertesaker' *Arsenal Magazine* January [Online] Available at http://www.arsenal.com/news/features/20160119/-sharing-the-responsibility-is-key-#g2Asd4TK9I22jy3L.99 (Accessed 29 June 2017).

Miller, Nick (2017) 'Brighton in Premier League: Knockaert, the Seagulls' star man', *ESPNFC.com* [Online] Available at http://www.espnfc.com/english-premier-league/23/blog/post/3106596/brighton-in-the-premier-league-hughton-knockaert-the-seagulls-star-men (Accessed 29 June 2017).

Murphy, Chris (2013) 'Mind over matter: Soccer's bid to train the brain', *CNN.com*, 26 February [Online] Available at http://edition.cnn.com/2013/02/26/sport/football/football-brain-mourinho-messi/ (Accessed 29 June 2017).

Musto, Robbie (2017) *NBC Premiere League Download: Pundits at the Lane*, [Online] Available at http://nbcsports.com/video/premier-league-download-pundits-lane (Accessed 29 May 2017).

Paul, Douglas (2008) 'Manager: Know Thy Strengths and

Weaknesses for Better and Worse', *FastCompany online*, 12 August [Online] Available at https://www.fastcompany. com/964627/manager-know-thyself-identifying-your-strengths-and-weaknesses-better-or-worse (Accessed 29 June 2017).

*Politico* (2017) 'Political Pulse', 6 June [Online] Available at http://www.politico.com/tipsheets/politico-pulse (Accessed 7 June 29, 2017).

Ponomareff, Lara, Lauren Pragoff and Matthew Dixon (2017) 'Customer Service Reps Work Best When They Work Together But Only 12% of Companies Let Them', *Harvard Business Review online*, 10 April [Online] Available at https://hbr. org/2017/04/let-your-call-center-reps-collaborate (Accessed 29 June 2017).

Quesenberry, Keith A. (2016) 'Social Media Is Too Important to Be Left to the Marketing Department', *Harvard Business Review online*, 19 April [Online] Available at https://hbr.org/2016/04/ social-media-is-too-important-to-be-left-to-the-marketing-department (Accessed 29 June 2017).

Ranieri, Claudio (2016) 'We Do Not Dream', *The Players Tribune*, 6 April [Online] Available at http://www.theplayerstribune. com/claudio-ranieri-leicester-city-premier-league/ (Accessed 29 June 2017).

Reid, Erin (2015) 'Why Some Men Pretend to Work 80-Hour Weeks', *Harvard Business Review,* 28 April [Online] Available at https://hbr.org/2015/04/why-some-men-pretend-to-work-80-hour-weeks (Accessed 29 June 2017).

Roeder, Oliver (2014) 'In 126 Years English Football Has Seen 13475 Nil-Nil Draws', *FiveThirtyEight.com*, 3 October [Online] Available at http://fivethirtyeight.com/features/in-126-years-english-football-has-seen-13475-nil-nil-draws/ (Accessed 29 June 2017).

Silver, Nate (2012) *The Signal and the Noise: Why so many predictions fail – but some don't,* New York NY: Penguin Press.

*Soccer.iSport.com* (2017) 'How to Communicate on the Soccer Field', [Online] http://football.isport.com/football-guides/how-to-communicate-on-the-soccer-field (Accessed 29 June 2017).

Smith, Peter (2017) 'Where would Riyad Mahrez fit in at Arsenal?',*SkySports Football News*, 5 June[Online] Available at http://www.skysports.com/football/news/11095/10904216/where-would-riyad-mahrez-fit-in-at-arsenal (Accessed 29 June 2017).

Stanzione, Vince (2014) 'The key to being successful? Act as if you already are', *The Millionaire Dropout*, [Online] Available at http://www.themillionairedropout.co/the-key-to-being-successful-act-as-if-you-already-are/ (Accessed 29 June 2017).

Sunstein, Cass R. and Reid Hastie (2015) *Wiser: Getting Beyond Groupthink to Make Groups Smarter*, Boston, MA: Harvard Business Review Press.

Treasurer, Bill (2013) 'Leaders Create Opportunity', *Association for Talent Development Human Capital Blog*, 23 April [Online] Available at https://www.td.org/Publications/Blogs/Human-Capital-Blog/2013/04/Leaders-Create-Opportunity (Accessed 9 June 2017).

Tuchman, Robert (2015) 'Five Reasons You Need to Work With Your Competitors', *Entrepreneur online*, 27 April, [Online] Available at https://www.entrepreneur.com/article/245375 (Accessed 9 June 29, 2017).

Vogelsinger, Hubert (1967) *How to Star in Soccer* New York, NY: Four Winds Press.

Wenger, Andrew (ND) 'Trust Your Instincts … If you can', *The Athlete Story*, [Online] Available at http://www.theathletestory.com/#!instincts/cb7s (Accessed 29 June 2017).

Wenger, Arsene (2016) *Arseblog* (2016) 'Interview with Roger Bennett, Men in Blazers', 4 October [Online] Available at http://news.arseblog.com/2016/10/arsene-wenger-meets-men-in-blazers-full-interview-transcript/ (Accessed 29 June

2017).

...(2017) 'Wenger: How to Improve Your Five-a-Side', *Four-Four-Two*, 3 May [Online] Available at https://www.fourfourtwo.com/us/performance/skills/wenger-how-improve-your-5-side (Accessed 29 June 2017).

Witz, Billy (2010) 'Jersey Swaps, a ritual with a story' *The New York Times*, 6 July [online] Available at http://www.nytimes.com/2010/07/07/sports/soccer/07jerseys.html?_r=0 (Accessed 29 June 2017).

# Further Reading

Other writings on soccer, management, leadership, society, and economics in addition to the works cited in this book that are worth checking out.

Leading: Learning from Life and my Years at Manchester United by Sir Alex Ferguson with Michael Moritz (2015) New York, NY: Hachette Books. One of the greatest managers of all time is now that Harvard Business School.

Conscious Business: How to build value through values by Fred Kofman (2013) Boulder, CO: Sounds True. Ari Gejdenson referred to this book a number of times during our conversation, it is an interesting read.

Mourinho by José Mourinho (2015) London, England: Headline Books. The "special one" explains why he is special.

How Soccer Explains the World: An (Unlikely) Theory of Globalization by Franklin Foer (2004) Harper Collins, New York NY. This is the soccer book everyone has heard of – a great read.

The Ball is Round: A Global History of Soccer (2006) by David Goldblatt Riverhead Books, published by Penguin Group New York, NY. This is pretty much the book on the history of soccer.

Finding the Game (2012) by Gwendolyn Oxenham St. Martin's Press, New York NY. A wonderful telling of playing pickup soccer around the world – it is also a documentary called Pelada. Oxhenham was a top college star who found a way to find the heart of the game by traveling the world with her boyfriend (also a top former college player) and finding games wherever they were. Pickup soccer is its own fascinating cultural world.

Among the Thugs by Bill Buford. (1993) Vintage Departures, a division of Random House, New York NY. Buford traveled with England's notorious soccer thugs – hooligans – for whom soccer is often an excuse to vent frustration and express local pride by wreaking havoc on everything in their path.

Silent Night by Stanley Weintraub (2001) A Plume Book published by Penguin: New York, NY. One of the few moments of hope in World War I was the legendary "Christmas truce." On Christmas Eve in 1914 on the Western Front, soldiers from both sides laid down their arms, climbed from the trenches, and played a friendly game of soccer. The soldiers exchanged gifts, sang carols, and buried their dead.

Soccernomics: Why England Loses, Why Germany and Brazil Win, and Why the U.S., Japan, Australia, Turkey – and Even Iraq – are Destined to Become the Kings of the World's Most Popular Sport by Simon Kuper and Stefan Szymanski (2009) Nation Books New York, NY. A little "freakanomics" and a little soccer, a fun read for those like to think about such things.

The Miracle of Castel di Sangro: A Tale of Passion and Folly in the Heart of Italy by Joe McGinnis 1999 Broadway Books, New York NY. The author of The Selling of the President 1968 (and a number of non-political books) traveled with, and wrote about a small-town team in Italy.

The Arsenal Yankee (2016) by Danny Karbassiyoon, Hamilton House, London. Danny was the first American to score for Arsenal's first team, but had his career cut short by injuries. He has since gone on to scout for Arsenal and co-found the online gaming company SWOL/Fury90. He is also a terrific guy. The book is a fun read and offers a perspective on what it can really be like trying to achieve at the very top level.

Changemakers Books
# TRANSFORMATION

Transform your life, transform your world - Changemakers Books publishes for individuals committed to transforming their lives and transforming the world. Our readers seek to become positive, powerful agents of change. Changemakers Books inform, inspire, and provide practical wisdom and skills to empower us to write the next chapter of humanity's future. If you have enjoyed this book, why not tell other readers by posting a review on your preferred book site. Recent bestsellers from Changemakers Books are:

### Integration
The Power of Being Co-Active in Work and Life
Ann Betz, Karen Kimsey-House
*Integration* examines how we came to be polarized in our dealing with self and other, and what we can do to move from an either/or state to a more effective and fulfilling way of being.
Paperback: 978-1-78279-865-1 ebook: 978-1-78279-866-8

### Bleating Hearts
The Hidden World of Animal Suffering
Mark Hawthorne
An investigation of how animals are exploited for entertainment, apparel, research, military weapons, sport, art, religion, food, and more.
Paperback: 978-1-78099-851-0 ebook: 978-1-78099-850-3

## Lead Yourself First!
Indispensable Lessons in Business and in Life
Michelle Ray
Are you ready to become the leader of your own life? Apply simple, powerful strategies to take charge of yourself, your career, your destiny.
Paperback: 978-1-78279-703-6 ebook: 978-1-78279-702-9

## Burnout to Brilliance
Strategies for Sustainable Success
Jayne Morris
Routinely running on reserves? This book helps you transform your life from burnout to brilliance with strategies for sustainable success.
Paperback: 978-1-78279-439-4 ebook: 978-1-78279-438-7

## Goddess Calling
Inspirational Messages & Meditations of Sacred Feminine Liberation Thealogy
Rev. Dr. Karen Tate
A book of messages and meditations using Goddess archetypes and mythologies, aimed at educating and inspiring those with the desire to incorporate a feminine face of God into their spirituality.
Paperback: 978-1-78279-442-4 ebook: 978-1-78279-441-7

## The Master Communicator's Handbook
Teresa Erickson, Tim Ward
Discover how to have the most communicative impact in this guide by professional communicators with over 30 years of experience advising leaders of global organizations.
Paperback: 978-1-78535-153-2 ebook: 978-1-78535-154-9

## Meditation in the Wild
Buddhism's Origin in the Heart of Nature
Charles S. Fisher Ph.D.
A history of Raw Nature as the Buddha's first teacher, inspiring
some followers to retreat there in search of truth.
Paperback: 978-1-78099-692-9 ebook: 978-1-78099-691-2

## Ripening Time
Inside Stories for Aging with Grace
Sherry Ruth Anderson
*Ripening Time* gives us an indispensable guidebook for growing
into the deep places of wisdom as we age.
Paperback: 978-1-78099-963-0 ebook: 978-1-78099-962-3

## Striking at the Roots
A Practical Guide to Animal Activism
Mark Hawthorne
A manual for successful animal activism from an author with
first-hand experience speaking out on behalf of animals.
Paperback: 978-1-84694-091-0 ebook: 978-1-84694-653-0


Readers of ebooks can buy or view any of these bestsellers by
clicking on the live link in the title. Most titles are published
in paperback and as an ebook. Paperbacks are available in
traditional bookshops. Both print and ebook formats are
available online.

Find more titles and sign up to our readers' newsletter at
http://www.johnhuntpublishing.com/transformation
Follow us on Facebook at
https://www.facebook.com/Changemakersbooks